Rabbit Adoption
FOR
DUMMIES®

by Connie Isbell

WILEY

Wiley Publishing, Inc.

Rabbit Adoption For Dummies®

Published by
Wiley Publishing, Inc.
111 River St.
Hoboken, NJ 07030-5774
www.wiley.com

For general information on our other products and services or to obtain technical support, please contact our Customer Care Department within the U.S. at 800-762-2974, outside the U.S. at 317-572-3993, or fax 317-572-4002.

Wiley also publishes its books in a variety of electronic formats. Some content that appears in print may not be available in electronic books.

Library of Congress Control Number: 2004111022

ISBN: 0-7645-7444-2

Manufactured in the United States of America

10 9 8 7 6 5 4 3 2 1

1B/RU/QZ/QU/IN

Publisher's Acknowledgements

Project Editor: Jennifer Connolly

Acquisitions Editor: Stacy Kennedy

Composition Services: Indianapolis Composition Services Department

Cover Photo: © GK & Vikki Hart/ Image Bank/ Getty Images

Cartoon: Rich Tennant, www.the5thwave.com

About the Author

Connie Isbell spent her childhood in rural New York State, where she experienced creatures of all kinds — domestic, farm, and wild alike. She carried this interest in animals and nature into her work as an editor and writer for *Audubon* magazine. She has also edited countless pet books, on everything from adopting an ex-racing greyhound to caring for rabbits and parrots. Connie now works from her home on the coast of New Jersey, where she lives with her husband and two daughters. In addition to her extremely supportive family, the author would like to thank Dr. Adam Christman DVM; Tracy Turner, Exotic Animal Veterinary Technician; and the New Jersey House Rabbit Society.

Table of Contents

The 5th Wave

By Rich Tennant

"We thought adopting a rabbit that already had some social skills made more sense."

Chapter 1

Ready, Set, Rabbits!

In This Chapter

▶ Finding out how to use this book

▶ Figuring out why adopt a rabbit

▶ Knowing their ups and downs

▶ Getting wild with rabbits

*W*elcome to *Rabbit Adoption for Dummies,* the best little reference for anyone who's looking to share their life with a rabbit. It's with good reason that rabbits are gaining popularity among pet owners. Their small size and quiet nature makes them an ideal choice for many; the fact that they can be housetrained is an added bonus (no need for long, late-night walks). But the sad truth is that when an animal becomes trendy or popular more people make impulsive or uneducated decisions to bring them home. When this happens to rabbits, they often end up in shelters or abandoned — not a happy ending. But with this book, and a bit of time and patience, you and your rabbit can live happily ever after.

First Things First: Using This Book

Rabbit Adoption for Dummies is a book I wrote for people interested in rabbits — whether you're a parent buying this book for you or your family or you're a teen buying him for yourself using your hard-earned cash. Maybe you just adopted a rabbit and need the essential scoop on getting set up, as well as general care information. Or, you may already have a rabbit and you need a refresher on the best way to take care of your pet or want to understand him better. Perhaps you're ready for a new pet but aren't sure if a rabbit is right for you and yours. If any of the above describes you, keep on readin'.

It's all in here — health and happiness, hay and hutches, tail twitches and nose wiggles. But this book is a reference, so you don't have to read it in order from start to finish. Begin with Chapter 4 if you need basic set-up information, flip to Chapter 6 if you're trying to learn rabbit-ese, or head to Chapter 2 if you're still on the fence about adding a rabbit to your family. (Although those of you who prefer to start at the beginning and read until you reach the back cover are welcome to do so. I'll never tell.)

As you read, keep an eye out for text in *italics*, which indicates a new term and a nearby definition — no need to spend time hunting through a glossary. And `monofont` points out Web addresses for additional information worth checking out. You'll also run into a few sidebars (the occasional gray box); although the information in the sidebars is good, it's not essential to the discussion at hand, so skip 'em if you want to. Also, because rabbits are living creatures, I disagree with grammarians about referring to any animal as "it." Instead, the use of "him' or "her" applies to both bunny genders, unless specifically noted otherwise.

While reading *Rabbit Adoption for Dummies*, be on the lookout for these icons sprinkled here and there:

This icon flags especially helpful hints to making life with your rabbit easier or making your rabbit healthier and happier. It highlights time- and money-savers, too!

Some things are so important that they deserve restating or summarizing. If you see this icon, it's there because I really think you should read this information.

This icon marks some of the most common mistakes rabbit owners make, along with some tips for avoiding them. Reading these may help you avoid some serious consequences.

You don't *have* to read the information next to the *For Dummies* guy, but I really think you should anyway. You'll see a lot of him in the sections where there's in-depth information — on health, for example. If you're in a hurry, give him a pass. But come back, please, for that little bit of extra information.

So, whether your bunny is already at home or is gazing at you through the bars of his cage at the rescue shelter, this book will prepare you for what's ahead. Life can be hard enough — let this book take the guesswork and goofs out.

Why Adopt a Rabbit?

Those who own or have owned a rabbit can talk for hours about the endless reasons to bring a rabbit into your life. They're great companions, have wonderful personalities, can learn tricks, and are lovable and curious creatures who deliver comfort, a bit of a challenge, and great joy.

When you adopt a rabbit from a shelter or similar situation, you're not just getting a pet, you're saving a rabbit from an uncertain fate. Tens of thousands are euthanized each year because rabbit rescues and shelters are overwhelmed with unwanted animals. In fact, by taking one rabbit home, you are making room for another at a shelter. You're also spreading the good word about rabbits as pets and showing others how it can be done — and done well.

Rabbits certainly need some help, that's for sure. So many of those who do end up in homes don't last for long, mainly because people really don't know what they're getting into when they bring one home. As wonderful as rabbits are, caring for them requires quite a bit of time and energy. They are not pets you can just feed and forget about. Plus, those people that are looking for a cuddly pet experience are often disappointed when they realize that rabbits really don't like to be handled.

When owners get frustrated and lose interest, they stop socializing with their rabbit, and the situation gets worse. Some people make the grave mistake of releasing their unwanted rabbit into the wild, into a dangerous, unfamiliar, and deadly situation. Others go the shelter route, a better option than the wilderness but not an ideal situation.

So, even if your intentions are good and pure in adopting a rabbit, you're not doing a rabbit any favors by bringing him home unless you are committed for life. For a rabbit, the only thing more difficult than being abandoned is being abandoned again when things don't work out. So here's a few of the reasons not to adopt a rabbit:

- ✔ You think that it would be so cute for your toddler to have a baby bunny to grow up with.

- ✔ Easter is just around the corner — what could be better than celebrating with your own little living Easter Bunny? How adorable!

- ✔ You'd like a pet, but you don't have much time. You're pretty sure that a rabbit is one of the easiest pets to care for.

- ✔ You have an empty corner of your yard and you think a rabbit hutch would look oh-so-quaint there.

Breeding and showing are reasons some people choose to have a rabbit. For the record, however, breeding is not for everyone — it's hard work and not a way to make some quick cash (even with those ever-prolific bunnies). As for showing, rabbits rarely benefit: traveling and living in small cages is not a recipe for a happy, healthy life. In addition, both show and breeder rabbits must be unspayed and unneutered, which means they need to be kept apart from each other, and unsprayed females will be at a high risk for reproductive cancers.

Discovering the bright side of bunnies

In addition to the painfully obvious — the cuteness, softness, quietness — rabbits shine in so many ways, some of which may surprise you. But, please, don't run out and find a rabbit just yet; I touch on some of the trickier aspects of rabbit ownership later in this chapter.

No dumb bunnies

The phrase "looks may be deceiving" certainly applies to rabbits. Behind those gentle eyes and fluffy exterior lies a very intelligent creature. In the wild, rabbits are survivors, outwitting and outrunning a host of hungry predators. They also live in complex social groups, with a hierarchal system of leaders and subordinates. Pet rabbits need to develop similar social relationships — whether with other animals or with their human companions (you'll have to figure out if you or your rabbit is the leader).

Rabbits are clever and inquisitive, and these traits make life with a rabbit fun and interesting. These same traits enable rabbits to solve all sorts of "problems," such as how to open doors, escape from hutches, tip over water bowls, and uncover boxes.

House happy

Rabbits make great house pets. Really, it's true. The days of outdoor hutches are nearing an end for many in the pet rabbit world. Given a cage and some room to roam, a rabbit can live very happily in most households. They can live with children and other pets, though best under supervision. They'll seek out your company — for some petting, snacking, watching television, or just hanging out.

Your house rabbit will enjoy having free reign of all or some of your house. Of course, a certain amount of careful bunny-proofing is a good — no, a great — idea (more on this in Chapter 4) With some patience and training, most rabbits can even be housetrained.

Tricks and treats

Much to the delight of their owners, it's possible — even likely — that a house rabbit can be trained to use a litter box. It will take some time and some effort on your part (your bunny won't just do it on his own), but the rewards are worth the effort. You can find helpful instructions in Chapter 6.

If you're jazzed about training, you can keep going with your rabbit. Rabbits can be taught their names and other words. A bit of training can even make life easier — like when you need your bunny to go into his cage or come when called. And although rabbits are certainly not going to respond to training like many dogs do, some rabbits can master such beginner "tricks" as sitting up or jumping on command.

Bunny love

Did you know that rabbits can show affection? Rabbits thrive on social interaction with their "family." If you are that family, and your rabbit has reached the point of really being able to trust you (remember how nervous they are about predators?), you're in luck. Licking, nudging, and cuddling are all signs that you are loved.

If you spend time watching your rabbit, you'll start to notice his special body language and what he has to say (more on this in Chapter 6). It's all part of understanding your rabbit and giving him the best life you can.

Flopsy's flipside

From the time we are born, adorable images of bunnies pepper our books, toys, wallpaper, movies. But living with a bunny is not always a fairy tale. Although all rabbits are different, there are some basic facts that anyone who is even remotely considering a rabbit should think about. Chapter 2 covers these realities in more detail, but here's a quick peek:

- ✔ You'll need at least one hour a day to properly care for your rabbit plus two to four hours for safe and supervised time out of his cage for exercise, play, and socializing.

- ✔ Young children and rabbits do not make a great team. Rabbits are fairly fragile creatures who can be harmed or even killed if handled improperly. On the other hand, a bite or a kick from a rabbit can hurt a young child.

- ✔ Rabbits housed outdoors face serious dangers — even death — from the elements. Rabbits should live indoors, according to most rabbit advocates. All rabbits need lots of time and room to exercise.

✔ Left to their own devices in an unprotected home, free-roaming rabbits are likely to dig, chew, and whittle their way through rugs, wires, books, and furniture. What about that super-soft fur? Yes, it sheds.

✔ Don't assume you'll have a happy family when you add a rabbit to a household of other pets. Cats, dogs, even other rabbits can pose a serious threat to one another's safety, unless introduced with care.

✔ Although the initial cost of adopting a rabbit is low, you'll be responsible for 8 to 12 years (yes, they can live that long!) of equipment, food, bedding, and medical expenses (which, in some cases, can be high).

✔ Rabbits are social creatures who need plenty of love and attention. They will not thrive if left alone for long periods. As much as they need companionship, however, most bunnies are not happy being held or cuddled.

Rabbits 101

Your pet rabbit is closely related to his cousins in the wild, so knowing a bit about wild rabbits and what makes them tick is a great way of understanding your own bunny.

On the wild side

Rabbits are *lagomorphs,* gnawing herbivorous mammals with two pairs of upper incisors, one behind the other. This order includes cottontails, jackrabbits, and European rabbits, from whom domestic rabbits are descended. They are famous for their prolific breeding, with as many as 12 *kits*, or baby bunnies, per litter and as many as 12 litters per year. Wild rabbits are buff to brown colored, to help them blend in with their surroundings. And they are fast — really fast; they can sprint at speeds up to 35 mph (56 kilometers per hour). Every one of these features is to help them survive (don't forget those radar-dish ears). But all that is not enough. Wild rabbits are preyed upon, hunted, and trapped in great numbers.

So rabbits try even harder to stay alive. They live in social groups called colonies, typically with as many as 15 rabbits. These rabbits hide under dense thickets in shallow depressions, or with European species, in a complex system of underground burrows called a *warren.* As part of a colony, a rabbit is protected by many sets of eyes and ears. Rabbits can thump their hind legs to warn others of danger (remember Bambi's little friend Thumper?), they avoid open, unprotected areas like the plague, and they are experts at squeezing into tiny holes for hiding. Sadly, it's still not enough. They are, simply, lunch.

Knowing what wild rabbits are up against, it's no wonder that they are so skittish and quick to run away. And it's no wonder that your rabbit feels the same way about a lot of things in your world — you, your kids, your other pets.

Happy together

Even if a rabbit colony isn't going to completely ensure a rabbit's safety, it's an important part of a rabbit's emotional well-being. Rabbits in a colony have a complex social order that helps them keep the peace. A dominant male, the *king buck,* and a dominant female, the *queen doe,* reign over the group; more submissive rabbits have their own roles in the society.

Rabbits use body language, sounds, and even scents to communicate with each other (they try to use that same language with people; more on that in Chapter 6). They show affection by grooming each other, and they form strong bonds. Bunny battling and marking (good old urine) are techniques used by the colony as its members work together to protect its territory.

Natural or annoying?

At first glance, a few natural rabbit behaviors just aren't suited to life in a human home. But the key word here is *natural.* Your bunny can't help himself — he isn't doing it just to annoy you (well, usually!). It's your job to see to it that he can live with all his bunny ways and you can live with your furniture, carpeting, and shoes. So here's where some rabbit-proofing and creative tactics can save the day (Chapter 4 covers this in great detail).

- ✔ **Digging:** There's no need to dig a burrow in your home, but it's a hard habit to break. Secure loose carpeting throughout the house (carpet fibers can seriously injure a rabbit) and cover your stuffed furniture; be sure to provide your rabbit with a box of safe digging material such as shredded paper.

- ✔ **Chewing:** A rabbit's instincts tell him to chew, gnaw, and nibble. Wrap electrical wires and exposed legs of wooden furniture; provide lots of cardboard tubes, woven mats, and untreated wood blocks for safe chewing.

- ✔ **Marking territory:** To keep other rabbits off their turf, wild rabbits spray their territory with urine. Companion rabbits, especially intact males, are at the mercy of their hormones and instincts so they do the same. Spay or neuter your rabbit. It's really the only way to save your home from this lovely little behavior (Check out Chapter 6 for more information).

Getting to the bottom of your bunny: Basic anatomy

A rabbit is as physically complex as he is socially and behaviorally. Think of your rabbit's body as a finely crafted piece of survival equipment (see Figure 1-1). Each organ and feature is engineered for a specific reason. If you're doing your job as a caretaker, your pet rabbit should be in a safer environment than in the wild, but those same survival instincts and strategies still apply.

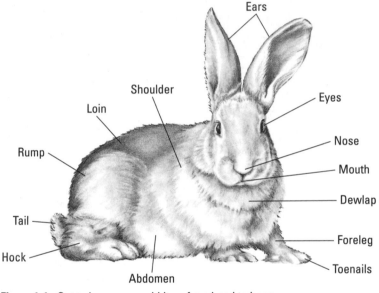

Figure 1-1: Get to know your rabbit — from head to buns.

A rabbit's ears are an obvious starting point in any discussion of anatomy. Those lovely ears, upright and *lop* (pointing downward), are used to collect sound and dissipate heat. Their shape and their ability to rotate make them especially effective at detecting approaching predators.

A rabbit's eyes are on either side of his head, which helps him to be on the lookout for predators in all directions; they have a blind spot right in front of them. Because they are *crepuscular,* that is, more active at dawn and dusk, their eyes are best suited to dim lighting.

It's cute and it wiggles — and a rabbit's nose doesn't get much rest. Like most animals, a rabbit's sense of smell is very acute; his sense of smell is one of the most important ways a bunny gathers information about the world. Rabbits smell their food, their predators, their babies, and other rabbits.

Because they're attached to his nose, a rabbit's whiskers also wiggle. More importantly, they feel things, judge distances, and help a rabbit move around. They have nerves in them so they should not be cut.

A rabbit's mouth works overtime to keep itself properly fed and fueled. His most important weapon? A set of serious chompers. These teeth grow throughout a rabbit's entire life; constant chewing and grazing on a proper diet of hay and other plant material can help keep them trimmed and healthy.

After those teeth do their business, food moves on its way through a rabbit's specialized digestive system. It's special in that it can cope with a wide variety of plant matter, some of which would be indigestible to most other herbivores. The logistics of this may not be terribly appealing at first, but most people eventually adjust to the idea that their rabbit needs to digest his food twice (the second time they do it, it has already been pooped out as a soft wet pellet). The waste products of the redigested food is finally excreted as dry pellets. You can read more on this in Chapter 5.

It may be the end of the line for our rabbit's digestive system, but the tail has a story of its own to tell. Sometimes a rabbit raises his tail to alert others of danger. When he shakes it, it's a sign of excitement, sexual or otherwise. A rabbit with his tail down doesn't have a care in the world.

To flee from predators, rabbits have been equipped with some seriously flexible bones and muscles. Zigzags, high jumps, and sudden twists in the air can make the difference in a life-or-death chase situation. Surprisingly, though, a rabbit's spine can be broken quite easily, even as a rabbit struggles against being held.

In the wild, a rabbit's coat protects him from the elements and helps the animal blend in with his surroundings (he's hiding from that predator again). Domesticated rabbits have been bred to have long hair or short hair, with a huge variety of coat colors and patterns. These variations have nothing to do with survival in the wild, but they can help a rabbit win a blue ribbon in a rabbit competition.

So many choices

Like many pets, rabbits come in all shapes, sizes, and colors. For some people, they're happy with whatever rabbit happens to be available, which is great — especially if you're going to an adoption shelter. Others have something more specific in mind. Potential adopters should remember, however, that personality is what counts, and that has nothing to with breed or color and everything to do with the individual rabbit.

The first and biggest difference in the bunny (and cat and dog) world is mixed breed or purebred. These and other differences, such as coat type, sex, ear type, age, and size, are discussed later in Chapter 3, which guides you through the process of choosing and adopting a rabbit.

Mixed breeds

A little bit of this and a little bit of that. A mixed breed is just that — a mix of different breeds that results in a unique, sometimes surprising, kind of rabbit. Unless you're looking for a rabbit for breeding or showing, mixed breeds make great companions. If you'd like to play detective you can probably find some clues about your rabbit's ancestry in his head shape, coat color and type, as well as his size and ear orientation (lop or not).

Purebreds

Although it had become common in the 1700s for people to keep rabbits as pets, it wasn't until the mid-1800s that rabbit owners began to develop specific breeds. Today, the American Rabbit Breeders Association, the governing body for the rabbit fancy in the United States, recognizes 45 different breeds of rabbits. Just like dog and cats, each rabbit breed has distinct features and common ancestors.

Born Free — And Staying That Way

If you've read this chapter, you probably know a lot more about wild rabbits than you did before. That's great. Again, what you know about them and their natural behaviors will certainly give you a leg up on understanding and caring for your own pet rabbit.

But just because we know a little something about wild rabbits doesn't mean that we should try to turn them into pets. Sure, you may see a mixed breed who looks a lot like the cottontail rabbit you see in hedgerow behind your yard, but they are not the same at all. Let wild rabbits stay wild (check out Chapter 3 for what to do with a wild bunny who you think has been abandoned).

Chapter 2

Checking Out Rabbit Realities

A rabbit certainly makes a great pet; after all, they're cute, not too big, and they won't wake up your neighbors. But although you need to consider whether a rabbit makes a good pet for you, more importantly, you need to consider whether *you* are the right person for a rabbit. The best time to ask yourself this question is now — before you've brought that bunny home or, perhaps, have made some serious mistakes with the one you're already shacked up with.

With rabbits, you need to contend with some basic truths — in terms of where they should live, how much time they require, how much money you'll need to spend initially and over the long-term, and how well your furniture matches up to bunny life. Other, perhaps trickier, considerations involve things such as how much patience you have and whether you think you have a pretty decent sense of humor. After all, no matter how much you prepare yourself, your family, and your rabbit for cohabitation, there's bound to be some unexpected moments. This chapter gives you an idea of what to expect of yourself, your time, your money, and your lifestyle when you choose to make a rabbit your companion.

Making a Hoppy Home

Not just any home will do for a rabbit. Rabbits require — and deserve — safe, comfortable, and inviting accommodations. So, first, you must decide where your rabbit will live. Up until fairly recently, people mostly kept their rabbits outside, more so for breeding and as a source of food (although it may not appeal to you, a great number of people still rely on rabbits for meat). However, people today are beginning to think quite differently about how domesticated rabbits should live.

Rabbits are great indoor pets. In fact, rabbit folk do not consider it cool or even humane to keep a rabbit outdoors in a hutch. Even in a well-made hutch, outdoor rabbits must deal with the threat of predators, inclement weather, and parasites. Rabbits have gone from livestock, essentially, to real companions who live inside their owners' homes — and not just in a cage in a home — many rabbits are litter-box trained and have free reign of a whole house, or a portion of one.

Considering the fact that rabbits need such freedom, you need to think about whether you have enough room for a rabbit to live, play, and exercise in. A rabbit needs a space to call her own, such as a cage, condominium, or exercise pen (see Chapter 4 for specific requirements), and she'll need a protected indoor area or outdoor run in which to roam and play safely.

Regardless of which of the below options you choose, always keep in mind that a rabbit is *not* the kind of pet who can live only in a cage. If you need that kind of animal, look into a tank full of fish, or maybe a hermit crab.

Living the indoor life

Extreme temperatures, weather conditions, and pesky preying varmints aside (more on those later), having a companion rabbit means sharing one another's company. Unless you're willing to camp out next to your rabbit's hutch, this kind of interaction is hard to achieve with an outdoor rabbit. One visit — or even two or three — during the day just isn't what your rabbit needs and deserves. In fact, many rescue groups won't adopt out a rabbit to someone who plans to keep her outside.

Consider the following advantages to keeping your rabbit indoors:

- ✔ You give her the chance to thrive on contact with other beings in your home such as other rabbits, other pets, and humans.
- ✔ You can get to know and appreciate her personality.
- ✔ You give everyone in the house, including your bunny, a chance to bond and build a relationship.

✔ You give your bunny a chance for a longer life by protecting her from a long list of health hazards.

✔ You can better monitor her health and detect any subtle signs of illness.

Roaming free

Not only can a rabbit live indoors, she can roam freely through a house or apartment and even be trained to use a litter box. A house rabbit will enjoy having a home base to use — a small room, an alcove — and a cage or pen (think of it like a den) for those times when she needs to be alone or catch some serious snooze. Being curious animals, however, rabbits like to explore and hang out with other family members, perhaps while watching television or reading.

To sneeze or not to sneeze?

Anyone who suffers from allergies understands how miserable and even debilitating they can be. So what if you're living happily with your rabbit, but you find yourself sneezing, wheezing, tearing up, and altogether unhappy about it? First, figure out what exactly you are allergic to — rabbit fur, rabbit saliva, rabbit hay, seasonal pollens, molds, and so on. If your allergies are truly rabbit related, you can take the following steps to reduce these allergens in your environment:

✔ **Handle With Care:** Wash your hands after handling your rabbit or her hay, and ease up on any face-to-fur cuddling and nuzzling.

✔ **Clean Sweep:** Dust, vacuum, and damp-mop frequently throughout your home to minimize those nasty allergens. Ideally, have someone who doesn't have allergies do the dirty work (or wear a mask when doing it yourself).

✔ **Off Limits:** Use baby gates, if possible, to limit your fur ball's presence in a room or two of your house. At the very least, keep your bedroom a rabbit-free zone.

✔ **A Clean Air Act:** Use HEPA (high-efficiency particulate air) filtration units, which can bring allergy sufferers great relief by pulling out fur, dust, and pollens.

✔ **High-gear Grooming:** Brush your rabbit daily and wipe her with a damp cloth to reduce fur allergens.

✔ **Doctor's Orders:** See if your doctor can prescribe medications to alleviate symptoms. Immunotherapy (allergy shots) may be an option also.

If this fails, and your health is jeopardized, you will need to find your bunny a new home. That's why you and your family need to spend some time with rabbits before making the decision to adopt — better to learn about any allergies now than have to find a home for your bunny later.

Some people are perfectly happy to give their bunny an all-access pass to their home. Considerable bunny-proofing is required in such cases, whether the bunny is free to roam night and day or just for a few hours in the evening. Others have a problem sacrificing their sofas and bedding to the ways of a rabbit; these folks are more likely to employ a more limited access approach (think baby gates) to certain areas of the house.

Surveying the scene

You need to consider all aspects of how keeping your rabbit indoors can affect your life. So think about the following needs and see how well a rabbit can fit into your life and home:

- **You need an appropriate home.** Make sure you have enough room — for some, this may mean an ample corner of a city studio apartment; for others, it may be an entire room (or rooms) — in your home for a rabbit. If you live in an apartment, make sure your landlord allows rabbits.

- **Make sure children are old enough to live safely with a rabbit.** All kids are different, but most rabbit advocates feel that eight years is generally when a child is physically capable of safely handling with a rabbit (See Chapter 5).

- **You need to be allergy free.** Find out whether anyone in your family is allergic to rabbits or rabbitty things like hay (See the sidebar "To Sneeze or Not to Sneeze?").

- **Be certain your other pets can live with a rabbit.** Although rabbits are social creatures and can enjoy the company of other pets, some house pets will instinctively prey upon and potentially harm a rabbit (see Chapter 5). Think about how your pets will react to a rabbit in the house.

- **Make sure you can live with some household obstacles.** You may need to set up barricades (baby gates, for example) to limit a rabbit's access to certain rooms.

- **You need to supervise a rabbit's free time.** Each day, you'll need to watch over your bunny as she roams, especially if she is confined to a cage during the day.

- **Be certain you can afford the expense of a rabbit.** You need to have money to feed and care for a rabbit, even if she requires potentially expensive veterinary care. (See this chapter's "Budgeting for a Bunny.")

- **You need to bunny-proof.** Consider what you'll need to change in your home to protect a rabbit from dangers such as toxic houseplants, electrical cords, and chemicals. Chapter 4 covers rabbit-proofing tactics in greater detail.

> ✔ **Make sure you can live with the likelihood that a rabbit will gnaw on a piece of your furniture or soil a rug.** Consider how you'll react when a treasured possession is damaged.

Housing your bunny outdoors

Out of sight, and perhaps out of mind, rabbits run a higher risk of being poorly socialized, lonely, neglected, and even forgotten about. In addition, because rabbits are a prey species, they learn to hide any symptoms of ill health. That means that a rabbit living outdoors will not demonstrate to you that she's sick, and you may not even know she's sick until you find her dead in the morning. A sensitive care-taker living with an indoor rabbit will be much more likely to detect the subtle signs of illness in time to get their rabbit to a veterinarian.

If indoor living is out of the question, consider the following:

> ✔ Do your residential zoning laws restrict rabbits?

> ✔ Will your neighbors or neighborhood association object to your building a hutch on your property?

> ✔ Do you have enough room in your yard for a large hutch that is safe, comfortable, and able to protect your rabbit's health (more on this in Chapter 4)?

> ✔ Do you have enough room for an enclosed exercise run?

> ✔ Do you mind that a rabbit probably won't respect your desire for an immaculate lawn and a lovely garden — after all, digging and chewing top the list of their favorite things to do?

Weathering the great outdoors

Even if you think you have an appropriate hutch, give some serious thought to the weather conditions in your area as well as who else is living outdoors Extreme cold and heat can stress a rabbit's system and even be fatal. Plus, because rabbits are programmed to be afraid of certain animals. A rabbit in an outdoor cage, no matter how secure it is, lives in constant fear of the dogs, raccoons, cats, and weasels lurking around. You may not see it happen, but a rabbit being attacked by a predator can literally die of fright.

Taking time outside

You need to make certain that if you keep your rabbit outdoors, you can guarantee her health and happiness. You must be diligent about her care, never feeling like it's okay to skip a feeding, a cleaning, an exercise session, or quality time. Loneliness can be devastating to a pet rabbit. So you must spend enough quality time with her. What qualifies as "quality time" varies, but most rabbits are just happy to be near you as you go about your household business (cooking, reading, paying the bills, watching television). However, exercise or play sessions are also a great way to spend time together (more on this in Chapter 5). Even if you get another rabbit to keep yours company, you'll still have to make a concerted effort to interact with them.

Keeping Track of Time

One reason that so many rabbits end up in shelters is that people have not done their homework so they have no idea how much effort is involved in caring for a rabbit. These are *not* low-maintenance pets. Rabbits require about as much work as a dog or cat, but it's often the kind of specialized care that people are not familiar with.

A rabbit is totally dependent on her owner. Simply put, if you don't have the time to care for a rabbit, she will suffer. If you are overwhelmed with other responsibilities, she will suffer. If you are in the middle of some sort of life event such as a new baby, a move into a new home, or a divorce, she will suffer. This doesn't mean that you should never have a rabbit; it just means that now may not be the right time to get started.

Preparing for the daily grind and gnaw

It takes about an hour a day to properly care for a rabbit. During this time, which can be broken up during a day, you need to feed, water, and groom your rabbit; you need to clean her cage or hutch. In addition, you need to give her at least two to four hours of exercise (see Chapters 4 and 5), which requires some supervision and interaction on your part. For many people, especially those who aren't thrilled about getting up an hour or two earlier every day, this free or out-of-cage time occurs in the evenings after work. And don't forget just hanging out — a devoted and happy rabbit is one who gets to spend a lot of quality time with her family (you and yours). A bunny mate, although she may help some, can not replace the affection you should provide.

If you've delegated some of the care-taking responsibilities to one or more of your children, ultimately, you need to accept the responsibility as your own, which means picking up where they slack off and making sure they care for the rabbit correctly. Even the most enthusiastic "helpers" may get distracted, disinterested, or just too busy to help.

Table 2-1 breaks down some of the duties of caring for a rabbit. Any attempt to skimp on these can result in problems for your rabbit; if indoors, your home and your family may suffer, too (like when you neglect to clean a litter box).

Table 2-1	The Duties	
Task	*How Often*	*How to Do It*
Feed the rabbit	Daily	Wash and cut fresh foods; wash out food bowls; add fresh hay
Change the water	Daily	Replace old water with fresh; wash out water dishes or bottles
Clean the litter box	Every 1 to 3 days	Change the litter and check for mishaps elsewhere in cage
Spot clean	Daily	Wipe dirty spots off cage; remove uneaten food and soiled bedding
Clean Cage	Weekly	Scrub cage with mild disinfectant; clean food and water bowls/ bottles
Play and exercise	Daily	Give rabbit at least two to four hours of exercise; play and be social

Preparing for the long haul

By taking excellent care of your rabbit and by keeping her indoors, you can expect your rabbit to live as long as 8 to 12 years. That's a lot of poop and pellets, you say? True, but more than that, it's a long commitment of your time and energy. A lot can happen in that amount of time, so think about where you may be in 10 years — off to college, married with babies, working full-time, retired and traveling, and so on. Make sure that you can accommodate your pet as your future changes. Because it's not that easy to find a new home for a rabbit (just ask anyone who volunteers at your local animal shelter).

Taking bunny on your travels

If road trips, cruises, and journeys abroad really tickle your fancy, consider just how much time you're away from home. On occasion, a rabbit can be left alone for longer than a few hours, but if you have more than that in mind, your pet needs someone else to care for her while you're away. You need to find someone with training, or you may even have to pay a professional pet sitter.

Don't be tempted to pack up your bunny's suitcase. Most rabbits are easily stressed and would prefer to stay right at home (if the vacuum cleaner bothers your rabbit, imagine what an airplane taking off would do).

Budgeting for a Bunny

Many people aren't sure how much money it takes to keep a rabbit, so they're often surprised at how quickly the expenses add up. Do your homework ahead of time and check out the impact your bunny may have on your budget.

Getting started

Initial startup costs can be deceiving, especially when people find rabbits who are being given away for free or next to nothing. When you adopt a rabbit from a shelter, the costs are also relatively inexpensive. With a shelter rabbit, the spaying or neutering fees are often included (if not, you'll need to arrange and pay for that yourself).

Here's where the bargains seem to disappear and costs begin to add up. You need housing that's comfortable and big enough for your rabbit (see Chapter 4 for more specifics); if you're getting a baby bunny, be sure to get a home that will fit her when she's fully grown, or you'll end up buying two. Expect to spend from $75 to over $250 for housing, from bare bones basics to deluxe designer digs. You also need accessories such as a food bowl and a hayrack, as well as supplies to keep them stocked. Don't forget the toys! Your rabbit will need them (factor in an additional $20 for these extras).

Buying a lifetime supply of carrots

Even after you've set up your basic supplies you have to maintain them. Remember, your rabbit may live to be 10 years old! More importantly, you have to add in costs for at least your rabbit's annual veterinary checkup (an annual well exam, for example, can range from $65 to $100, depending on where you live), and more visits should she have health problems. In many cases, the combined cost of exams, treatments, and medications can be formidable.

One of the most important things you can do for your bunny's health is to feed her a healthy diet, so you need to factor in the cost of food. You'll spend about $2 a day to feed the average rabbit, including quality hay, rabbit pellets (if a part of the diet), and fresh produce. I cover more of this in Chapter 5.

Mixing Children and Rabbits

Few things appeal to children more than fuzzy little creatures with big eyes. And for most kids, rabbits are up there at the top of the He's So Cute list, right alongside kittens and puppies. We adults like to think that we're teaching our children about responsibility when we let them have pets, but rabbits are not designed to be teaching tools.

Face it: Children can be a bit loud, a bit rough, and a bit strong willed. They may not listen when you ask them to be quiet, pet gently, or "leave that poor bunny alone." On the other hand, children can be kind, caring, and gloriously awestruck by the wonders of nature. To create a loving relationship, teach by example and let your child see how caring and kind you are toward your rabbit. However, to protect both your child and your rabbit you should:

- ✔ Always supervise any contact.

- ✔ Not assume that your child can care for a rabbit by herself.

- ✔ Teach a child how to gently pet a bunny without picking her up.

- ✔ Watch your rabbit's body language to know when she's stressed.

- ✔ Never let a child chase a rabbit.

- ✔ Teach your child that bunnies are frightened by loud noises or voices.

Doubling Up: Thinking About Two?

Like their wild descendants, pet rabbits crave a bit of company, a social life even. Though they are not very active during the middle of the day, left alone for hours at a time, day after day, a rabbit may feel lonely, dejected, and not at all like a happy camper. But not every pet rabbit needs another rabbit in order to live a full life. Rabbits who live indoors have a social advantage in that they are surrounded by human activity, whether it's the television, someone cooking dinner, or someone on the phone. An owner who spends a few hours a day around his rabbit may be all that the rabbit needs to be well socialized and happy.

However, a rabbit may need a partner if:

- ✔ She lives indoors but is caged during the day while her owners are at work.

> ✔ She lives alone in a large outdoor hutch (other drawbacks of this situation are discussed earlier in the chapter).

For the most part, two rabbits means twice the expense and work. You'll need to buy and clean two cages (or some other form of housing) and two sets of accessories. You'll also need to buy and prepare twice as much food, and you'll have to clean up after two sets of digestive systems. Some of this may seem nit-picky, but it all adds up — particularly when you're talking about pricier expenses such as medical bills and supplies.

Given a little time to get acquainted, most rabbits can get along with other rabbits, but to ensure a happy pairing, be certain to spay and neuter. Not only does this prevent unwanted litters, but it also eliminates the hormonal issues that cause territorial marking and aggressive behaviors (see Chapter 7).

Preventing Breeding

Those that love rabbits can be tempted to breed them; after all, what's the only thing better than one rabbit? Two rabbits (or three, or four, or seven . . .). But just because rabbits are prolific breeders doesn't mean that yours have to be, too. Following, I give you some very serious reasons *not* to breed your rabbit:

> ✔ **Rabbits, rabbits, everywhere:** Animal shelters and rabbit rescue group are flooded with homeless bunnies and rabbits. The harsh reality is that many are destroyed each year because they are not wanted. Any breeding of rabbits contributes to this tragic story.
>
> ✔ **Health hazards:** Females who aren't spayed are more likely to suffer from a variety of health problems (See Chapter 7 for health concerns related to breeding).
>
> ✔ **Cashed out:** Even if you were to breed a desirable purebred — there won't be much, if any, profit left after you subtract the money it takes to care for the parents and the kits. And when it comes to mixed breeds, take a look at your newspaper's classifieds — people can't give them away, let alone sell them.

You may think breeding is the right thing to do if you have a remarkable purebred rabbit, or a winner in the world of rabbit shows. But it is still complicated, expensive, and will result in yet more rabbits in a world in which rabbits are euthanized every day.

Chapter 3

Adopting a Rabbit

*W*hen you're ready to welcome a rabbit into your life, you have several options to choose from when you start looking. Getting a new pet is very exciting, but keep your wits about you during this process — and remember all the realities of rabbit ownership covered in Chapter 2. You can deal with buyer's remorse when you choose the wrong model of television, but dealing with a living, breathing creature is not so simple.

Finding Your Source

For a culture that's so crazy about pets (we buy them sweaters, gourmet foods, professional grooming sessions), Americans live with the reality that millions of animals are destroyed each year because they have nowhere to go and no one to care for them. Rabbits are no exception to this tragic tale. Given the number of abandoned rabbits and those who face euthanization, anyone considering a rabbit should first think of adopting one in need of a home (check out Chapter 1 for more on why there are so many rabbits waiting to be adopted). So this section gives you the basics on where and how to adopt your new bunny. Depending where you live and what resources are in your area, you should have little problem finding a homeless bunny ready to settle down, but if you can't, I discuss other routes you can explore, too.

Rescue me!

Because so many abandoned rabbits need homes, look for your bunny at shelters and through rabbit rescue groups. These people care for the ever-growing rabbit population until the bunnies find good homes.

Keep in mind that regardless of how overtaxed these animal shelters and rescue groups are, they are not in the business of doling out rabbits to folks not prepared to care for them properly. Rabbits require specialized care and a commitment of time and energy, both daily and over the long-term (Chapter 2 details those responsibilities).

Going the rescue group route

Because of the overwhelming needs of homeless rabbits, rescue groups have sprouted up across the country to take up the cause. Often, these not-for-profit groups of individuals focus on rescuing unwanted rabbits and those about to be destroyed in shelters. Their ultimate goal, of course, is to find good lifelong homes for these rescued rabbits.

The House Rabbit Society, formed in 1988 (see the sidebar, "Speaking for Rabbits," in this chapter), leads the way in rabbit advocacy today. With a network of chapters across the country and world, dedicated volunteers provide foster homes for bunnies until they can be adopted. Other rabbit rescues are out there, too; an Internet search will list many.

Speaking for rabbits

Bunny history was changed forever in 1988. By forming the House Rabbit Society, a progressive group of seven rabbit lovers began to spread the word about the joys and needs of pet rabbits. Before then it was nearly unheard of to keep a rabbit inside, let alone one who was free to roam throughout your house. Thanks to the HRS, owners are now better able to live with and care for their house rabbits. The nonprofit organization is also committed to finding homes for homeless or abandoned rabbits; a network of chapters throughout the world and a rabbits-only shelter in California works to foster rabbits and pair them with caring humans. To find a chapter in your area or learn more about HRS contact them at 148 Broadway, Richmond, California 94804 or check out their Web site at www.rabbit.org.

Although individual groups may have their own variations, a typical adoption would work as follows:

- ✔ You find and contact a local rabbit rescue group, whether through the House Rabbit Society or some other means.

- ✔ Before you even see any rabbits you'll be screened by a volunteer. This is the part where they'll go over what will be expected of you as an adopter (note that the HRS and many other rescue groups require that rabbits live indoors). They'll also ask questions to find out what kind of life a bunny will live in your care. In some cases, a volunteer will visit your home.

- ✔ If the group feels that you are a good candidate, they'll tell you about available rabbits in the area. In most cases, the rabbits are living in a volunteer foster parent's home, and they'll help coordinate a meeting.

- ✔ You'll meet the rabbit and the foster parents. In many cases, the whole family is required to attend; this way, the rescue volunteer can observe everyone and talk more about rabbit care. While you're there, you can watch the bunny go about his business and, most likely, interact a bit.

- ✔ You should talk to the foster parents about the rabbit's personality and needs. After all, they've been living with this rabbit (and have probably lived with many others), so they'll have good insight to tap into.

- ✔ If the group approves you for adoption and you've found a good match, you'll pay a fee (around $65) and, in many cases, sign an adoption agreement. After you're home, the foster parents or someone from the group will check up on the rabbit and see how things are going. They may also be available for support as you get settled and beyond.

Find out as much as possible about a rabbit's health history. Rescue groups will have a good handle on any health problems, and the rabbits typically go through some sort of health exam, but take a good look for yourself (you can find more information on see the signs of an unhealthy rabbit later in this chapter).

Searching in shelters

The good people at animal shelters around the country, which may be run by private groups or local governments, do their best to find homes for abandoned or neglected dogs, cats, rabbits, and a host of other pets. Although some shelters don't accept rabbits, those that do likely have mixed breeds as well as some of the more popular breeds such as the Dutch, the Netherland Dwarf, and the Holland Lop.

But not all shelters are the same or even have rabbits available. Review not only the following differences between shelters, but also how to handle the adoption process through the different types of shelters you may discover:

- ✔ Some shelters screen potential adopters and include spaying and neutering in their typical adoption fees (to prevent future unwanted litters from ending up back at the same shelter). Be prepared to be screened (as long as you remember the care and commitment advice in Chapter 2, you shouldn't have problem with this); to take home a healthy bunny, unable to add to the ever-growing bunny population (because the rabbit is spayed or neutered); and to pay an adoption fee of anywhere from $35 to $95.

- ✔ Some shelters do not screen or spay or neuter bunnies, charging only a nominal adoption fee (sometimes of just $1). Be prepared to screen yourself to be sure you're ready for a bunny (see Chapter 2) and to pay to spay or neuter your bunny, which can cost from $100 to $350.

- ✔ Some shelters euthanize unadopted rabbits after a certain period of time. Other shelters, called *no-kill* shelters, keep all rabbits until they're adopted (unless there are serious concerns about health or aggression). However, no-kill shelters that accept rabbits are rare, so be sure to call shelters to be advised of their specific policies on rabbits.

If a shelter has rabbits, it will have perfectly wonderful companion rabbits. Consider the following when going the shelter route in search of your bunny:

- ✔ **Call ahead.** Not all shelters have rabbits all the time.

- ✔ **Tell it like it is.** If shelter staff asks you a series of questions to be certain that you'll provide a rabbit with a good home, tell them about your family, other pets, schedule, and so on.

- ✔ **Check out the shelter bunnies in person.** Keep in mind any qualities you envisioned in your pet (long or short hair, large or small, feisty or quiet), although love at first sight sometimes overrules those preconceptions.

- ✔ **Hang out.** Many shelters have getting-to-know-you areas for potential owners to spend time with and observe the candidates. Shelters can be pretty chaotic (think 45 barking dogs), so this may only give you a glimpse of what the rabbit will be like in your home.

- ✔ **Open your eyes.** Look for signs of illness or health problems (I discuss more about particular health problems to watch for later in this chapter). Discuss your concerns with the staff.

Here comes Peter Cottontail: The downside of the Easter bunny

Easter is a time of wonder and joy for children everywhere, but for those running rabbit rescue groups and shelters Easter is nothing to celebrate. In their holiday excitement many people impulsively buy a super-cute pet bunny for their children. But a family's enthusiasm quickly wanes after those little bunnies turn into adolescent rabbits. After all, these are *real* rabbits — not animated or stuffed — and they don't dig being held or handled roughly.

It's not long before children lose interest and parents tire of the more-than-anticipated care requirements. Enter those rabbit rescue groups and shelters. This annual deluge of unwanted rabbits is an event that organizers and volunteers begin to dread early in the year. Faced with an overwhelming number of rabbits, many shelters are forced to euthanize — certainly not what the Easter Bunny had in mind.

Bunny breeders

Although the bunny world discourages showing bunnies, if you're ready for a rabbit and want to show him, you need to find a purebred rabbit. You can find excellent purebreds through shelters and rescue groups; however, rescues spay and neuter all their rabbits, which would disqualify the rabbits from showing, and rescues won't allow rabbits to be adopted for show because of how showing can negatively affect a bunny. So, if you really want a show-quality breed of rabbit you need to purchase one from a responsible breeder.

If you're looking for purebreds because you're thinking about breeding them, see Chapter 2, which goes over some misconceptions and ethical issues related to hobbyist rabbit breeding.

Because this book is about *adopting* a rabbit, check out the following reasons to reconsider buying from a breeder.

- ✔ A breeder's rabbit will be more expensive than others.
- ✔ When you buy from a breeder, you're missing out on the chance to rescue a rabbit from a shelter.
- ✔ Breeders typically cannot offer insight into the challenges of living with an indoor rabbit.

If you're still in the market for a purebred rabbit, you should definitely find a reputable breeder, one that takes excellent care of his rabbits. Look for a rabbit *fancier,* a person that breeds to the point of excellence, who knows about his rabbits' bloodlines (and is able to provide a *pedigree,* a registry recording of three or more generations), and probably has showing experience.

If you're looking for such a responsible breeder, the following can guide you in the right direction:

- ✔ The American Rabbit Breeders Association (ARBA) is the commander in chief of purebred rabbits and their owners. A national organization that registers purebred rabbits and sanctions rabbit shows, its Web site lists the national clubs for the 45 different ARBA recognized breeds. You can contact the individual breed clubs to find breeders throughout the country; however, just because a breeder is linked to the ARBA site is not a guarantee of quality or responsibility — do your own research to be sure.

- ✔ Through your County Extension office, you can find out if any local 4-H clubs have ongoing rabbit programs. Although 4-H programs are designed for young people, they are often run by or associated with local rabbit breeders.

- ✔ A rabbit veterinarian will likely work with or know of reputable breeders in your area. They will also be more likely to know of any health concerns inherent with certain breeds.

Unfortunately, not all breeders are reputable, and many rabbits suffer because of a lack of proper care. For this reason, it's so important to do your research and rely on the trusted resources listed above.

Even if you've done your homework and you're confident in your choice of breeder, you should still be on the lookout for any signs of health problems (more on that later in this chapter).

Combing the classifieds

Open any local newspaper's classified ad section and you're likely to see one, two, or a dozen ads selling bunnies.

Yes, you can find rabbits to buy in the classifieds. Although it may be less expensive than other options, it won't include any spaying or neutering services. You also can't be certain what you'll be getting in terms of health, socialization, pedigree (if any), even size (tiny bunnies can grow into little rabbits or big rabbits). Plus, you're encouraging the hobby of rabbit breeding, which is one reason there are so many homeless rabbits waiting to be adopted from shelters.

If you do go the way of the classifieds, proceed with caution. Certainly examine the rabbit for any obvious sign of ill health (more on that later in this chapter). If possible, take a look at the rabbit's housing and living conditions to see that they are clean and well-equipped. Finally, ask if you can have your veterinarian check out the rabbit before you seal the deal (if you don't have one, get one quick! See Chapter 7.)

Looking into retail rabbits

Although adopting rabbits is very important (see the earlier section on adopting), some people choose to buy a rabbit from a retailer. If you're one of those people, keep the following in mind:

✔ You may not be able to determine several factors, such as where they came from, how healthy they are, what kind of pet they will make, and who their parents are (that is, are they purebred or mixed breed?).

✔ You're unlikely to find a bunny expert working at a pet shop, so you can't be sure what kind of information you may be getting.

✔ Those looking for a show-quality purebred be warned — just because a rabbit is "purebred" doesn't mean he is show quality; he may be a fine pet-quality purebred instead.

✔ You're missing out on the chance to rescue a rabbit from a shelter situation.

Fortunately, many pet shops now sponsor adoption events, when they invite local shelters or rescue groups to bring their bunnies in for the day or the weekend. This is a great chance for potential owners to find out more about rabbits — and take care of their pet supply needs.

Choosing the Right Rabbit for You

Is your *perfect* rabbit out there? Is it possible that there's just one rabbit who's right for you? It's unlikely. Even those people who had and lost what they considered to be the "best rabbit in the world" often find themselves shacked up with another equally wonderful rabbit sooner or later.

Whether you have a particular rabbit in mind or you're still considering your options, you can learn a lot about the different types of rabbits out there, which will help you get through the sometimes confusing, sometimes emotional, process of choosing a rabbit.

Mixing it up

Purebred rabbits come in several shapes, sizes, colors, and coat types, but for someone looking for a companion rabbit, a mixed breed makes a fine choice. They are readily available, less expensive than a purebred, and they're often ready to be adopted from shelters and rescue groups (although you can often find purebreds in shelters and rescue groups also). Because mixed breeds are a combination of two or more breeds, you can't always be sure what you're getting, but you can find clues to your bunny's heritage in breed descriptions that can help solve the mystery. Remember, however, that a rabbit's personality and capacity to love is not found in his heritage, so his looks and background really don't matter when it comes down to it.

Even if you're not looking for a particular breed, you should consider two factors when thinking about getting a rabbit: size and coat type. Your rabbit needs to fit into your home (spacewise) and your life (timewise).

Size

Size does matter when it comes to a pet, even a relatively small pet like a rabbit (rabbits can weigh from 2 to 20 pounds/.9 to 9 kilograms, as shown in Figure 3-1). The bigger the rabbit, the more space he requires (and more food, too!), which is an important consideration, especially when a rabbit will be sharing your digs. In searching for a rabbit, you're likely to see these terms used to describe bunny sizes:

- ✔ A **dwarf** rabbit weighs 2 to 3 pounds (.9 to 1.3 kilograms).

- ✔ A **small** rabbit weighs 4 to 5 pounds (1.8 to 2.3 kilograms).

- ✔ A **medium** rabbit weighs 6 to 7 pounds (2.7 to 3.2 kilograms).

- ✔ A **large** rabbit weighs 8 to 9 pounds (3.6 to 4 kilograms).

- ✔ A **giant** rabbit weighs more than 9 pounds (over 4 kilograms).

Figure 3-1: The dwarf breed of rabbit (on the right) is not much bigger than an apple, while the giant breed (on the left) truly towers over the pair.

Although you're bound to meet bunnies who are an exception, size can also matter when it comes to a rabbit's personality. For example, larger rabbits are known to be calm and easygoing (and even though they weigh more they can also be easier to handle); smaller rabbits, on the other hand, tend to be a bit more nervous and temperamental — and fragile. You can find out more about rabbit personalities based on their breed later in this chapter.

Coat types

Rabbit coats are soft and furry. They also come in two types: short-hair and longhair. There are three types of shorthairs — normal, rex, and satin; angora coats are longhaired.

All rabbits, even the shortest of the shorthairs, require some basic grooming. But because grooming a longhaired rabbit can take up a big chunk of your time, it's a good idea to think about how much time you have for brushing before you bring one home (look for more specific guidelines in Chapter 5).

The following list gives you a general idea of how much grooming each type of coat takes:

 ✔ **Normal:** Most rabbits have normal fur, which is about 1 inch (2.5 centimeters) long with a fine undercoat; coats such as this require weekly brushing sessions.

- **Rex:** Found only on Rex rabbits, rex fur is shorter than normal fur and feels extremely plush and velvety; coats such as this require weekly *gentle* brushing.

- **Satin:** Shiny and lustrous, satin fur gets its special looks from fine, somewhat translucent hair shafts; satin fur is about the same length as normal; coats such as this require weekly brushing sessions.

- **Angora:** It's hard to miss rabbit breeds with angora fur, which is fluffy and grows 2 to 3 inches (5 to 7.6 centimeters) in length; this type of coat requires daily brushing year round.

Considering all the factors

In this section, I discuss several other factors you may want to consider when choosing your rabbit, such as sex, age, and personality. Everyone has an opinion as to how much these factors affect how good of a pet a rabbit makes. However, regardless of those opinions, the best advice is to be informed and spend time with the rabbit first to see how well he fits in with your personality and family.

Boy or girl

Rabbit folk have plenty of opinions about whether males or females make the best pet, but the only opinion that really matters is yours. This is particularly true if you — and you should — have spayed or neutered your rabbit. By doing so, you minimize the hormonal surges that cause males to be aggressive and territorial (a nice way of saying that they spray urine all over the house) and females to be preoccupied with having baby bunnies. That said, neutered males and spayed females make equally fine pets.

Little lost bunny

As cruel and foolish as it may sound, some people believe that a domesticated rabbit will be able to fend for himself in the wild. Not true — rabbits abandoned in the wild by their owners are unlikely to survive for long. If you come across a stray bunny in your neighborhood or yard, first check to be sure that he is a domestic rabbit (obvious signs are lop ears or an all-white, spotted, or angora coat). Watch the rabbit's behavior; a wild cottontail is not likely to approach you or your home. Next, unless you can safely catch the rabbit (unlikely), you'll need to call in the experts or try to trap the rabbit using a humane trap (the House Rabbit Society offers guidance on this). If you call your local humane society in to capture the rabbit, you may be able to adopt him once they're convinced that his owners aren't looking for him.

Considering character

Whenever you can, try to observe a rabbit in his home environment. Watch how he interacts with other rabbits and how he reacts to humans. What's the rabbit like? Playful? Timid? How does he respond to handling? These are all clues into his personality. If you have a rabbit at home consider how the two may get along; two aggressive males, for example, may not be the best pairing.

Some breeds are known to have particular personalities — easygoing, high-strung, timid — but all rabbits are individuals, so it's best to spend as much time as you can with a rabbit before you bring him to your home.

Young or old

If you've given the age of your rabbit any thought, you may have been tempted by images of adorable baby bunnies dancing in your head. Yes, bunnies are incredibly cute, but they aren't always that sweet and docile. Before long, they are in the midst of adolescence angst (this is when most of those Easter bunnies wind up in shelters). Owners who can weather the storm (and the mischievousness, chewing, and digging) with patience while the teenager outgrows this stage will be rewarded with a fine companion.

If you have your heart set on a baby bunny, one that is between 9 and 12 weeks old requires some training. A more mature rabbit may be calmer and have some training behind him, which could make your life easier. Although he may take a little longer before he trusts you and feels comfortable, his loyalty will be worth the wait. Typically, there are more older rabbits than babies in need of adoption.

Watching for signs of an ill rabbit

Wherever you look for a rabbit, be certain he is healthy. Most importantly, try not to let your emotions get the best of you — only bring home an ill or special needs rabbit if you are prepared for the extra money, work, and potential heartache involved. Take note of the following:

- ✔ Listlessness is a sign that a rabbit is not feeling well for some reason.

- ✔ Eyes and nose should be free of discharge; look inside ears — a brownish, waxy residue can be sign of ear mites. These problems can be treated by a vet, but it will likely be your responsibility to arrange and pay for it.

- The rabbit should be clean and free of odor; in particular, make sure the hindquarters are clean, without traces of diarrhea.

- Feet should be without sores.

- If a rabbit's upper teeth overlap the lower teeth, it may be due to a problematic congenital defect called *malocclusion*. Because a rabbit's teeth grow continuously, they must meet evenly in order to grind down properly (malocclusion can be controlled with proper veterinary care).

- A rabbit's coat should be soft and shiny, with no bald spots or mats; be wary of a rabbit who feels too thin.

Chapter 4

Bringing Home Bunny

. . . .

. . . .

inally! The moment you've been waiting for — your bunny is coming home! As with any pet, you'll need to take care of a few things before you hang up that "Welcome" sign on your door. If you read Chapter 2, which touched on some of the realities of rabbit ownership, you've had a chance to think about where your rabbit will live and what you'll need to do to prepare for her arrival. If you haven't, go back, take a peek, and then read on.

Shacking Up or Heading Out

The first and most important decision you have to make about your rabbit is where she will live. Will you have a house rabbit or an outdoor rabbit? Times have changed since the old days of outdoor hutches, and more and more people are discovering the joys of living with an indoor companion rabbit. This section explains why keeping your rabbit indoors is rewarding for both yourself as well as your rabbit.

Getting to know you . . .

Because they share the same living space, house rabbits and their owners really get to know each other, which is great. A rabbit's social well-being is dependent on this companionship. No matter how many visits a caretaker makes to his outdoor rabbit, this rabbit is less likely to bond with him.

One of the best parts of this bonding is that it can happen at any time of the day. Your rabbit may sit next to you while you watch your favorite show at night. Or maybe while you chat on the phone, fold laundry (those towels are fun to hide under), or read a book. Don't forget mealtimes — many bunnies take great pleasure in "dining" with their caretakers (yes, rabbits can beg!).

Not to be overlooked, house rabbits are tons of fun. They love to play and act silly, whether with you, another rabbit, or by themselves. You're a lucky person to be a part of the antics — to be able to observe the dancing, racing, and joyful binky-ing (more on these in Chapter 6). Even the best-intentioned owners are challenged to spend enough time playing with their fresh-air bunnies.

Protecting from predators

House rabbits are protected from outdoor predators. Even in the best made hutch, predators such as raccoons, snakes, and cats can injure and even kill a rabbit.

Even if they aren't actually harmed by a predator, an outdoor rabbit lives in constant fear of what may be lurking about. This stress wears on a rabbit's system. In the worst cases, a rabbit can even be scared to death by a predator's presence. When you keep a rabbit indoors you can feel good about taking that fear out of your rabbit's life.

Keeping better care of your rabbit

House rabbits are not subjected to the same health problems that trouble outdoor rabbits. Inclement weather, parasites, temperature changes (both heat and cold), and diseases all take their toll on an outdoor rabbit. They are exposed to more viruses and bacteria, and so are more susceptible to illness.

Most importantly, outdoor rabbits may suffer from undetected illnesses, often until it is too late. House rabbits live longer because their caretakers are able to watch their droppings and urine, monitor their appetite, and spot subtle behavioral changes that signal illness.

Living with House Rabbits

To create a successful indoor habitat, a bit of preparation is in order. You'll need to gather some basic equipment, do some clever rabbit-proofing, and muster up some patience.

The House Rabbit Society, the pioneering force behind the house rabbit movement (see Chapter 2), provides incredibly valuable insight for new rabbit owners. The volunteers who serve as foster parents for homeless rabbits have been through it all, and they have tips for most any situation.

Shopping before bunny gets home

Well before your bunny's arrival, you should purchase and set up the equipment and supplies she'll need. Rabbits are a bit nervous to begin with, let alone when they are being taken to a new place, so the more you can do ahead of time the better her transition will be.

You can shop for what you need at a pet supply store, over the Internet, or through a catalog.

Getting your bunny her own home

Your rabbit's housing is the first and most valuable purchase you'll make, so choose wisely. Keep in mind that rabbits crave protection from predators and danger, and a cage is one of the most important ways you can provide a safe "nest" for your pet. Even if your rabbit will be free to roam about the house or parts of it, she will still need a cage to call her own.

Look for a cage made specifically for rabbits, but beware of poor quality commercial cages that will not provide your rabbit with the space or comfort she deserves. An example of a basic indoor cage is shown in Figure 4-1. You can explore other options (discussed later in this chapter), such as custom rabbit "condos" and pens. Keep in mind the following guidelines when making your selection:

- **Size:** Your rabbit needs plenty of room, and she should be able to hop, stretch, turn around and stand up without bumping her ears on the top. A good rule to follow is to provide at least 1 square foot (.1 square meters) of space for every pound (.5 kilograms) of rabbit. So if your rabbit weighs 6 pounds (2.7 kilograms), she'll need at the *bare minimum* 6 square feet (.5 square meters) of space, which is a cage that measures 2 by 3 feet (.6 meters by .9 meters). Be certain your rabbit has enough head room — about 2 feet (.6 meters) — to stand up on her hind legs. Keep in mind that you'll also need room for accessories such as nesting boxes and food containers, so don't skimp on size. In addition, the longer a rabbit is caged, the larger the space needs to be.

- **Design:** Look for a wire-sided cage (with mesh no larger than 1 by 2 inches/2.5 by 5 centimeters) with a large side door for easy access. Choose a cage with a solid floor (you can add a grass mat or piece of carpeting for comfort).

✔ **Room to grow:** If you are getting a young bunny be certain you buy a cage that's big enough for her to grow into. If you've picked a mixed breed of unknown heritage, err on the safe side and go for a bigger cage — it may save you from buying a second one when she outgrows the first.

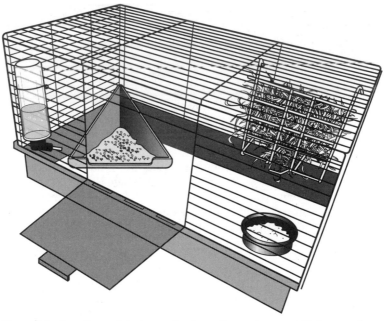

Figure 4-1: A well-appointed cage, for those times when a rabbit just needs to get away from it all.

Thinking outside the cage

If possible, consider the excellent alternatives to standard cages that are available. Many smaller companies, often run by dedicated rabbit lovers, make wonderful housing options geared to suit a rabbit's needs (see Chapter 8). Just as important, such companies know what makes a rabbit caretaker happy — smart design, quality construction, good looks, ease of use. These alternatives are quickly gaining popularity for those who share their homes with house rabbits.

✔ **Rabbit condos** are single-, double-, or triple-level homes for house rabbits. Levels are typically connected by ramps, to give bunnies access to different floors. Rabbits love the extra room for stretching and hopping about, yet they can still feel safe and secure.

✔ **Exercise pens** are one of the least expensive, most flexible, and most humane ways of housing a rabbit; they are especially useful for those owners who don't want to keep their rabbit in a cage, but they need a way to confine their rabbit while they are away from the house or asleep.

Getting into gear

A cage (or condo!) alone does not make a happy home, so you'll need to accessorize with some important bunny gear. To save some hassle, veteran rabbit owners often suggest that you buy two sets of everything — one to use while the other is being cleaned. Be sure to grab the following gear before you bring your bunny home:

✔ **Food containers:** Heavy crock bowls made especially for small animals work best to foil your rabbit's attempts to chew or tip hers over. Make sure that they are the proper size for your rabbit (not too deep that your rabbit can't reach into it).

✔ **Water supply:** A gravity water bottle (seen in Figure 4-1) is a good way to keep your rabbit flush with clean, fresh water. A heavy crock (to foil those tipping temptations) full of water is another option.

✔ **Hay rack:** Rabbits require a constant supply of Timothy, oat, or brome hay for roughage in their diet, which helps with digestion (more on nutrition in Chapter 5). A proper hay rack like the one in Figure 4-1 will keep your bunny's hay in place — and off the floor of the cage.

✔ **Litter box:** Yes, your rabbit can use a litter box! Buy one that that fits nicely in your rabbit's cage (look for one like in Figure 4-1 that nestles in a corner); make sure it's large enough for her to sit in comfortably. Buy at least one more to use outside of the cage or wherever the rabbit will play. The larger the house or running space, the more boxes are needed.

✔ **Litter:** Your rabbit won't have much success with her litter box without the litter. Pelleted bedding made of materials such as paper and aspen control both moisture and odor. Avoid clay, cedar, and pine litters, which can be harmful.

✔ **Nest box:** A cozy nest box will really make your rabbit feel protected in her cage. Look for them in rabbit supply catalogs or on the Internet; even easier, give your rabbit a cardboard box with holes cut into it (you can replace it when it gets too chewed up.

✔ **Padding:** To make your rabbit feel extra cozy and comfortable, add a piece of carpet or rug to the cage floor (if your rabbit likes to eat carpeting, opt for a grass mat instead).

> ✔ **Grooming tools:** As long as you're shopping, pick up the grooming brushes you'll need to keep your rabbit's coat looking and feeling fine (wooly breeds need daily brushing with a slicker brush). More on grooming in Chapter 5.

Finding the right toys

Rabbits love to tunnel, chew, hop, dig, and shred, and there are plenty of toys on the market to help encourage those natural urges (they'll also redirect your rabbit from those not-so-fun activities, such as chewing on your furniture). Look into toys designed for rabbits that need to chew, as well as the balls, bells and other toys made for cats, parrots, and even babies. Of course, any toy you give your rabbit should be safe — no loose parts, toxic coatings, or soft plastics that can be swallowed.

Several companies sell excellent toys that are specifically geared to rabbits. Busy Bunny, Cats & Rabbits & More, and Leith Petwerks (you can find them on the Internet) were started by rabbit lovers, so they know of what they sell. Check out their offerings to see what plaything may appeal to your rabbit's personality (baskets and grass mats are especially popular).

You can also try some of these homemade versions:

> ✔ Cardboard box (cut out "doorways") to hop over or hide in

> ✔ Paper bag to crawl inside (add some shredded paper or hay)

> ✔ Wicker baskets (untreated) for hiding, digging, and chewing

> ✔ Cardboard paper towel and toilet paper rolls to nudge, toss, and chew

> ✔ Shallow box or basket of shredded junk mail or newspaper for digging

> ✔ Old phone book for shredding and chewing

Setting the scene

Just as important as the cage you get is *where* you put it. You could buy the best rabbit cage in the world, but if you place it in the wrong spot in your home, your bunny will not be happy. Again, the idea is to keep your new companion comfortable, healthy, and safe. Consider the following as you scope out your home for your rabbit's locale:

> ✔ Look for a place where your rabbit will have company at times but will also be able to be alone (a busy hallway is a bad idea, but a nook off the kitchen, the living room, or den just may work).

- Rabbits are very sensitive to drafts and dramatic changes in temperature. Do not put the cage near windows or doors to the outside, or next to heating or air conditioning vents.

- A basement or any other damp area of your home is not a good place for your rabbit.

- Your rabbit will do well with a nice well-lit spot for her cage, but direct sunlight can cause her to overheat and suffer; similarly, a spot near a radiator or woodstove will be stifling and dangerous for your rabbit.

- Because they are sensitive to loud noise, keep your rabbit's cage away from televisions or stereos.

- Your rabbit needs to have a sense of day and night. If you can't put the cage in a location that is dark for about eight hours a day, cover it instead.

Saving the sofa: rabbit-proofing

You should consider what it takes to rabbit-proof your home before you get a rabbit and certainly before you bring one home. Doing so saves yourself trouble down the line and you may even save your rabbit's life. Fortunately, plenty of owners have done this ahead of you, so you can take advantage of their clever ideas to make your job much simpler.

Take a moment to think about why you need to rabbit-proof in the first place. You'd like to have a rabbit live in your home (a great idea!), but a rabbit is a rabbit, no matter where she lives. There's not much you can do to change the way a rabbit naturally behaves (read more on this in Chapter 6), so instead you need to work it out so they can be rabbits and you can still have your home.

Although some people do give their rabbits access to their entire house, many compromise and give a rabbit a cage in a room or part of a room, and at certain times of the day allow her to roam around with her owner.

Outwitting your rabbit

In rabbit-proofing you have two jobs: protect your rabbit from harm and protect your home from your rabbit. It's as simple as that. Think about how much time your bunny will be out of her cage and where she will be allowed to go, and then consider the following tactics:

✔ Put yourself in your rabbit's place, down on the floor if you can, and take a really good look around your home, one room at a time. Parents sometimes use this approach when their babies start creeping around and getting into trouble (outlets, cabinets, VCRs). The same applies to bunnies.

✔ Supervise your rabbit any time she is out of the cage. Even if you've done a great job of rabbit-proofing, there's always the chance you missed something or your bunny has outwitted *you* and gotten into trouble. This is especially true with a new or young rabbit.

✔ Most people who aren't willing to turn over their entire house to a rabbit limit their bunny's access by using baby gates. That way, a bunny can leave her cage and hop around, but stay out of rooms with rugs and other prize possessions. Portable exercise pens (see Figure 4-2) are another way of giving a rabbit some extra space without sacrificing your stuff (she'll still need supervised time out for serious exercise).

Figure 4-2: For some, a portable exercise pen provides the perfect blend of space and safety.

Chomping down on chewing

Rabbits can't help themselves when it comes to chewing. Unfortunately, it's not so good for your home and its contents. In some cases, chewing can even be deadly. Keep the following chewing hazards in mind as you go about your business of rabbit-proofing:

✔ Electrical wires and telephone and computer cords are extremely appealing chew items. At the least, such nibbling will render your phone useless. A more tragic result is electrocution. The solution? Cover all wires with plastic tubing from a hardware or aquarium store. You can also purchase spiral cord wraps or wire concealers that mount to walls.

✔ House plants look like food for rabbits, and they have no way of knowing which green leafy things are good to eat and which ones will make them sick. The solution? Remove those plants that are toxic to rabbits (the House Rabbit Society has a list) and hang or put up high any safe plants you'd like to keep.

✔ If a rabbit feels the need to gnaw, and the only available victim is the leg of your table, the table is a goner. The same holds true for baseboards, chairs, etc. The solution? If you can't supervise your rabbit every moment, you can wrap the items in heavy plastic or block your bunny's access to them.

Carpeting may not tempt your taste buds, but for a rabbit with an urge to chew, it will do just fine. Rabbits have an uncanny knack for finding loose edges of carpeting; however, when ingested, the fibers can block the digestive system. The solution? Cover vulnerable areas of carpeting with heavy furniture, woven grass mats, or plastic rug protectors. Again, you can also limit your rabbit's access to rooms with carpeting.

Although it can't replace any of the above measures, you should give your rabbit plenty of other safe things to chew on (see "Finding the right toys" earlier in the chapter).

Dealing with a digger

Digging, another natural behavior, does wonders for a rabbit in the wild when she needs to dig a burrow or hide from a predator. In your home, however, digging means nothing but trouble — for you, your carpeting, and your upholstered furniture.

Protect those digable targets before your rabbit gets into trouble. For carpeting, secure loose edges and cover with sheets of plastic carpet protectors. To keep your rabbit from getting under beds and upholstered furniture and burrowing up into the soft underside, block the entrance with cardboard or wood. Cover sofas and beds to keep them from being dug up and destroyed.

It can't replace any of the above measures, but you should also give your rabbit her own place to dig — a shallow box or basket of shredded junk mail, newspapers, or magazines to dig in to her delight.

Hiding out

In the wild and in your home, a rabbit will feel the need to hide under objects and in tiny nooks and crannies. In your living room, this means you could lose your bunny behind a sofa; in your kitchen your bunny could become trapped behind the refrigerator. Use your bunny brain to spot these little temptations and block them as well as you can.

Taking care of dust bunnies

One of the best things you can do for your rabbit is to provide her with a clean and healthy home. The added benefit is that your own home will stay clean and free of rabbit-related problems such as odors and waste. Trust me, rabbit urine is very strong and can be quite offensive.

Many people find it helpful to make these tasks part of a regular routine, just like other household tasks.

- **Daily:** Remove any uneaten fresh foods from cage; clean food bowls and water bottles; tidy up in general.

- **Every one to three days:** Clean the litter box. Change the litter bedding and wipe up stray waste in other areas of cage; take note of any unusual droppings that would indicate illness.

- **Weekly:** Thoroughly clean the cage. Scrub off debris and use a mild disinfectant (mix the 1:10 solution of bleach and water yourself); soak for 30 minutes; rinse and dry completely. Do the same with water bottles and food bowls or wash in dishwasher.

Keeping indoor rabbits happy

A contented rabbit is less likely to act aggressively or out of boredom. But a few toys and some time out of the cage won't be enough to maintain a bunny's bliss. Use the following ways to keep your bunny's happiness blossoming:

- **Companionship:** Rabbits are incredibly social creatures, so you need to give them a social scene (you, your family, other pets); this is especially true when you have a single rabbit. Most rabbits are satisfied to just be part of the family, which makes your job simpler.

- **Exercise:** Not only does exercise keep a rabbit happy, it keeps a rabbit healthy. A rabbit cannot get proper exercise in her cage (unless, maybe, it's a *really* huge deluxe condo cage). Chapter 5 gets serious about fitness and fun, but keep in mind that your rabbit will need at least two hours a day of exercise. Like humans, rabbits may need some coaching, so encourage yours with play, toys, and tricks.

✔ **Field trips:** A journey to the great outdoors can be a real treat for an indoor rabbit, especially one who needs some exercise. I discuss rabbit-proofing your yard later in this chapter goes over some serious safety concerns such as poisonous plants, so take extra precautions when your rabbit is outside and certainly never leave her unattended while she's exploring your yard.

Caring for Outdoor Rabbits

Although more people than ever before are sharing their homes and their lives with companion rabbits, this kind of living arrangement may not work for everyone. There are many excellent reasons to keep your rabbit indoors, but if you're not able to, you can take certain safety measures to make sure your rabbit has a good life outdoors.

It's a wild world

Domesticated rabbits are just that — domestic, which means they are not able to survive in the wild. Consider the following threats to an outdoor bunny's life and think about what it will take to make your rabbit safe, comfortable, and healthy.

✔ **Predators:** Even the best-made hutches can be infiltrated by rabbit-hungry predators such as foxes, dogs, cats, raccoons, even snakes and weasels. Wire mesh can be bent or broken, locks can be opened (those rascally raccoons!). Just the sound or sight of a predator can cause a rabbit to panic and injure herself; rabbits can even be frightened to death. On top of it all, the constant fear of prowling predators causes unnecessary stress on a rabbit's sensitive system.

✔ **Weather:** Outdoor rabbits are exposed to extreme weather conditions and temperature changes, all of which can be harmful. Even a well-made hutch may not offer enough protection from rain, wind, cold, and heat.

✔ **Longevity:** Outdoor rabbits do not live as long as indoor rabbits. Several factors are responsible for this, the main one being that an owner is not able to observe an outdoor rabbit often enough and consistently enough to notice the subtle signs of ill health. In addition, outdoor rabbits are prone to dangerous parasites such as fleas and mites — all of which can lead to serious and even deadly health problems.

Given these threats, keep in mind that this is not a strictly black-or-white issue: indoors or outdoors. Alternatives exist for those willing to "think outside the hutch," so to speak. How about housing your rabbit in a hutch on a screened porch? A garden shed can be adapted to fit a hutch and an attached exercise pen. Some people go for a more flexible arrangement, where they have an outdoor hutch but they bring their rabbit indoors at night (when predators are more likely to be on the prowl), during inclement weather, or when they have health concerns.

Having the best hutch on the block

The rabbit hutch is the foundation of any outdoor living arrangement. Whether it is made of wood or metal, on legs or near the ground, a hutch is a cage-like structure for housing outdoor rabbits. Figure 4-3 is an example of a pretty basic medium-sized hutch. Keeping in mind that your goals include comfort and safety, you can consider this a starting point to work up from.

Figure 4-3: A hutch, though not exactly a castle, can be a home for a rabbit.

Hutches come in different shapes, designs, levels of quality, and price ranges. And, you guessed it, it's your job to figure out what works best for you. Whatever hutch you choose needs to be well built, secure, safe for your rabbit, and weatherproof. Read on to get the basics.

Sizing up the hutch

Although your bunny should have an attached exercise run or daily supervised out-of-hutch experiences, she will spend much of her time in her hutch. This is her habitat, her world, really. It needs to be big enough for her to do most of the things she needs to do: sleep, play, hide, eat, drink, dig, chew, pee, and poop. As you'll read in Chapter 5, rabbits who are not active enough suffer from health problems such as obesity.

Your rabbit's hutch also need to have room for her "stuff" such as a litter box, a nest box, and food bowls (see more on gear earlier in this chapter). If her quarters are cramped, you'll be more likely to have problems keeping up with your rabbit's urine and feces, which is unhealthy.

To give you an idea of the bare minimum cage size your rabbit will need, you can figure on 1 square foot (.1 square meters) of space for each pound (.5 kilograms) of rabbit. For example, you'll need at least 9 square feet (.8 square meters) for a 9-pound (4-kilogram) rabbit. Logically, you'll need to double the space when you have two rabbits (you'll need at least 6 square feet (.5 square meters) of space for two 3-pound (1.4-kilogram) rabbits. Again, these are the *minimum* requirements.

Delving into design matters

From the traditional wood and wire hutch to more elaborate bunny buildings, hutches range widely in style and design. Although an attractive hutch adds some interest to your yard or garden area, consider function first and foremost. Keep the following guidelines in mind as you consider the available options:

- ✔ **Height:** Look for a hutch that is several feet off the ground, especially if you live in a cold area (a cage close to the ground is more likely to get cold and damp). This height factor will make your cleaning tasks easier because you won't have to do as much bending.

- ✔ **Material:** Hutches made of wood and hutches made of metal each have advantages and disadvantages. Wood hutches are more traditional and popular; owners like how they insulate against heat and cold, but they can be difficult to clean. Wooden hutches also deteriorate over time and are chewed on by rabbits (many are also made of redwood, which is toxic to rabbits). Hutches made of metal usually last longer than those made of wood. Although they are easy to clean, they have the disadvantage of retaining heat in the summer and cold in the winter.

- ✔ **Weatherproofing:** A hutch must be able to protect a rabbit from the elements. Look for a pitched, waterproofed roof to keep rain and snow out; consider a hutch that has solid or canvas side panels to protect from wind-driven rain.

✔ **Flooring:** The floor of a hutch needs to serve two purposes: protect a rabbit from the elements and allow waste to drop down and out of the rabbit's living quarters. Look for a hutch that is at least one-third solid flooring (smooth wood or wood covered with a piece of carpeting or a linoleum type of material), which will protect your rabbit's feet from cold and disease. Smooth wire should make up the remainder of the floor; be certain mesh is no larger than ½ inch by 1 inch (1.3 by 2.5 centimeters).

✔ **Protection:** A hutch should provide security from predators as well as the elements. Three sides of the hutch should be constructed of solid material (remember those prowling predators and how nervous they make a rabbit feel); the fourth side should be wire mesh to give your rabbit a view outside. To prevent your rabbit from getting stuck and to keep predators from reaching in, the mesh should be no larger than 1 by 2 inches (2.5 by 5 centimeters — chicken wire won't work). Look for a hutch that has built-in hiding spots, or fit your hutch with a nest box or two for when your rabbit needs to get away from it all. Of course, locks should be strong and secure.

Finding the right location

Where you put your rabbit's hutch is just as important as the hutch itself. Take a good look at your yard and think about which spot will work best for your rabbit. It would be nice if this location made for an aesthetically pleasing arrangement, but that shouldn't be your primary concern; instead, consider the following:

✔ **Temperature:** Temperatures above 80 degrees Fahrenheit (27 degrees Celsius) can be dangerous for rabbits, so be wary of any area of your yard that gets direct sunlight, especially during hot weather seasons. Choose a spot that is shaded but not dark and gloomy. Keep in mind that no amount of shade can protect a rabbit against the hot temperatures common in some areas of the country.

✔ **Circulation:** Your rabbit needs fresh air, but too much wind can take its toll on your rabbit's health. Choose a spot that is shielded from the wind, but that will allow fresh air to circulate.

✔ **Wind:** Although rabbits seem to handle cold better than heat, choose a spot where your rabbit won't be exposed to chilly winds. If you live in a cold climate install a heating system or move your rabbit indoors for the winter.

✔ **Moisture:** Dampness, whether from humidity or rain or snow, is harmful to a rabbit's health. Place your hutch in a spot that is protected from these elements to keep moisture out; proper ventilation helps keep a hutch dry and cozy.

✔ **Noise:** Rabbits are easily stressed by loud noises and too much activity, especially during the day when they like to nap. Think about the noise from cars, kids, barking dogs, and neighboring activities when scoping out a spot.

✔ **Access:** The spot you choose should be easy to get to and easy to see from inside your home. You'll make many trips out to your rabbit's hutch to care for and visit her — the more pleasant this experience is the better. You'll also want to keep an eye on the hutch (even from a distance).

A hutch for everyone

After you figure out what kind of hutch you need and where you'll put it, you can go about the business of getting one. No matter where you look for one or what type you end up with, a hutch is not a home unless it is well built, safe, and comfortable.

Buying a bunny hutch

For most people, the easiest way to get a hutch is to purchase one from a catalog, from a pet or farm supply store, or on the Internet. Again, for the reasons listed in the section on size, buy your rabbit the largest hutch you have room for and can afford. A hutch is a very important investment, so be certain you are getting your money's worth in terms of quality. If you're looking in person, check to see that it has a strong frame and is made of quality materials.

One of the best ways of finding a good hutch is to talk to people who have them. You're certain to get an earful of advice and loads of tips from people who are either satisfied or not thrilled with their own purchases. This kind of research can save you a lot of time and money.

Building a hutch from scratch

It probably takes more skill and time than most people have, but some owners choose to build you're their own hutches. Because you'll have to pay for quality materials, you're not likely to save much money, but you can build the hutch the way you want it. Hutch kits can be purchased on the Internet and through some catalogs, and the American Rabbit Breeders Association (www.arba.net) also sells building plans.

Safety is a real concern with some homemade hutches; be sure yours is secure and follows the hutch guidelines listed earlier in this chapter.

Keeping it clean

Just because you're not sharing the same house doesn't mean you can slack off on keeping your rabbit's home clean and sanitary. The following cleanup schedule helps keep parasites and other nasties away and keeps your bunny happy and healthy.

- ✔ **Every day:** Dispose of your rabbit's droppings from under the hutch (use it in compost or bag it up as garbage). Wash out food bowls and water bottles. Remove soiled bedding from nest boxes and replace with new bedding.

- ✔ **Weekly:** Thoroughly scrub and disinfect the hutch using a 1:10 mixture of bleach and water (relocate your rabbit to a secure spot first!). Wait until the hutch is completely dry before returning your rabbit to her sparkling home.

Rabbit-proofing your yard

As with rabbit-proofing your home, your work in rabbit-proofing your yard is two-fold: to protect your rabbit and to protect your yard. In both cases you may want to consider limiting your bunny's activities to a penned-in area. Again, taking care of a few precautions ahead of time saves you hassle and potential heartache later.

Protecting your rabbit

At first glance, your yard or garden may seem like the perfect place for a rabbit — spacious, with lots of plants and places to explore. Take a closer look, from your rabbit's perspective if possible, and you may see a much less inviting scene. Check for the following:

- ✔ **Possible escape opportunities:** Rabbits are true escape artists and can find and squeeze through tiny holes in walls or fences. If given the opportunity, they may also dig their way under a fence and into trouble.

- ✔ **Poisonous plants:** The lovely plants in your yard may not be safe for your rabbit to eat. The House Rabbit Society publishes a list of poisonous plants that you should keep away from your rabbit. Also, unless you've gone organic, you may have used garden fertilizers or pesticides that can be harmful.

- ✔ **Dangerous spots:** Be on the lookout for any potentially dangerous spots that your rabbit will likely explore — the stack of old paint cans behind the shed, the box of old garden tools next to the garage.

Protecting your yard

Wherever your rabbit is, she's likely to act on her natural urges to chew and dig. If you spend a lot of time grooming your lawn and nurturing your plants, you may not be thrilled with the results of your rabbit's little garden party. To keep your bunny happy and your yard intact:

- Always supervise your rabbit outdoors.
- Use an exercise pen to limit your bunny's access to the yard.
- Give her her own spot to dig or a box of dirt or sand to burrow through if you don't want your rabbit to dig in your vegetable bed.

Keeping outdoor rabbits happy

Regardless of where a rabbit lives, she will be happier and healthier when her owner goes out of his way for her. A little extra effort and time can make a huge difference in your rabbit's quality of life.

Extra amenities

Face it, living outdoors just isn't as easy as living indoors. Rabbit rescue groups and online rabbit chat groups can share great ideas for making an outdoor rabbit's life the best it can be. Add a heating system for those chilly nights, use insulation to keep things cozy, treat your bunny to some cool air in the summertime, and employ some clever means of keeping your rabbit's water from freezing in the winter. Your rabbit is worth it.

Companionship

Whether she's by herself or living with a partner, an outdoor rabbit still needs socialization. Without the constant activity of a household, a rabbit is likely to become bored and lonely. Spend time visiting and playing with your outdoor rabbit every day, as often as possible. This is an especially good idea because you'll need to be on the lookout for any signs of illness, parasites, and so on.

Exercise

Just because a rabbit is outside doesn't mean that she's getting exercise. In fact, unless your rabbit is allowed out of her hutch, she's probably getting little exercise at all. Remember that all rabbits need at least two to four hours of exercise every day. Make it part of your schedule to let your rabbit loose every day — encourage her to run, play, and get silly with some toys.

Homeward Bound

When the time comes to bring your bunny home, take care to make the experience as stress free as possible.

A royal rabbit chariot

Most rabbits do okay during short car trips, but you can make the experience as pleasant as possible. Most importantly, you'll need a proper carrier and set up before you hit the highway. Use a cat-sized airline carrier, *never* a box, and secure it to keep it (and the rabbit inside!) from bouncing around in the car.

Unless you're traveling a great distance, keep the rabbit in the carrier for the entire trip; add some hay or bedding for a bit of comfort. Be sure the car is cool enough, and never leave your rabbit in direct sunlight or alone in the car.

Making a smooth move

After you're home, you can slowly work on getting your rabbit acclimated to her new habitat. It may take time, probably at least a week, before she'll seem to relax a bit.

To make things easier on you and your newcomer, take care of any necessary rabbit-proofing and have your cage and supplies set up ahead of time. Put her cage in a quiet spot; she'll probably appreciate having a nest box to hide out in or a covered section of cage to steal away to. Try not to startle your rabbit with any sudden movements or loud noises, and certainly wait a while before bringing other pets around (See Chapter 6 for more on how rabbits deal with dogs, cats, and other animals).

Meeting the family

Even before your rabbit arrives at home, you should talk to the other members of your household about what will be happening and how your rabbit will feel. Children, especially, need to be told that the rabbit will be frightened at first but will eventually be able to be gently petted (see Chapter 2 for more information on interaction between children and rabbits). Keep a close eye on young children, who will no doubt be curious and excited about their new friend.

Remember that your bunny is dealing with a big change. Be patient and give her some time to adjust. Again, this process often takes a week or more. Be calm but friendly with your new companion, and she'll soon give you signs that she's settling in.

Chapter 5

Caring for Your Rabbit

● ●

In This Chapter

▶ Feeding your rabbit a nutritious diet

▶ Maintaining a bunny's fit figure

▶ Getting a grip on handling your rabbit

▶ Brushing up on grooming

● ●

Anyone who thinks that a rabbit can be taken care of like a cat or a dog is in for a bit of a surprise. Rabbits are special creatures, with equally special care requirements. The more you know about their nutrition, exercise, and grooming needs, the easier it will be to keep your rabbit healthy and happy.

Feeding Your Bunny's Belly

To get the nutrients they need, rabbits need to eat a lot of low-calorie, high-fiber plant material. To do so, wild rabbits spend several hours a day foraging, chewing, and generally *grazing* on whatever plants are available. With a rabbit in your care, you are responsible for planning, purchasing, preparing, and serving up a delightful menu of grass hay, fresh greens, water, a bit of fruit and other veggies, and in some cases a pelleted food.

Although rabbits are grazers, they are most active in the early and later parts of the day. This is when they'll want to eat, so you should feed them two meals a day, both morning and evening (with hay available at all times).

Rabbit nutrition is the subject of much discussion and debate, often leaving new owners at a loss for how to fill their bunny's bowl. The following are simply guidelines; a trusted rabbit veterinarian can help ease any concerns you may have about your particular furry friend. Never make any sudden dietary changes — your rabbit's sensitive digestive system simply can't handle it.

Understanding rabbit digestion

What your rabbit eats will form the foundation for good health and a long life. Domesticated rabbits live much differently than their wild cousins, but they should still eat a similar diet: all plants and no meat, eggs, or even bugs. All rabbits are *herbivores,* which means they eat only plants. The plants that wild rabbits eat vary a bit from those you feed your rabbit, but the goal is the same — to keep the body running efficiently.

To get the maximum nutrients out of the plant material they eat, a rabbit's digestive system has some interesting features. Like another famous herbivore, the horse, a rabbit can digest some pretty fibrous foods — hay, grass, and twigs. As these foods move through a rabbit's digestive system, they are passed into the *cecum,* a part of the intestines where the hard-to-digest fibers are treated to some hard-working microorganisms that turn them into small, soft, nutrient-rich pellets called *cecotropes.*

Here's where things get even more interesting. Several hours after the rabbit eats his meal, these cecotropes pass through the anus, and the rabbit instinctively knows to eat them up right away (that's why you won't find them lying around in litter boxes — if you do, there may be a problem with your rabbit's diet; see Chapter 7.). These lovely little power pellets are then digested once again, this time emerging as the hard, dry, round pellets you do — and should — find in your rabbit's litter box (cecotropes are shiny and a bit stinky).

All of this plant fiber provides more than just rabbit nutrients; without it, things don't move as quickly or smoothly as they should through the intestines and disease and gastrointestinal problems develop (more on these in Chapter 7).

Hay isn't just for horses

After you understand how critical fiber is to a rabbit, you can appreciate the value (but probably not the taste!) of a good pile of hay. Basically, hay is dried plant material, usually a grass or a legume. For a companion rabbit, this hay is the perfect thing to graze on — it's high in fiber (good for an efficient and hairball-free digestive tract), with a bit of nutritional value, but it's low in calories (so your rabbit won't get fat from grazing on it all day).

So which hay? The average mature rabbit — one who receives a varied diet of fresh foods — should be given an unlimited supply of grass hay. Many caretakers stick with timothy hay; others prefer to mix in Brome, oat, or orchard. The legume hays, alfalfa and clover, are too high in protein, calories, and calcium for most companion rabbits; they should be avoided, except in special cases that I cover later in this chapter.

Fresh is best when it comes to your rabbit's food, and hay is no exception. Fresh hay should be green (but not dark-green alfalfa), sweet smelling, and not dusty. You can find hay at feed stores, from local farmers, or online (see Chapter 8); pet stores may also carry it, but check its quality. Only buy what you need for a month or two and store it in a cool dry place.

A constant supply of fresh hay is one of the best ways to keep your rabbit healthy. Rabbits often pick through hay to find what pieces appeal to them, so add small handfuls and replace daily. A hay rack keeps hay contained for easy snacking; rabbits will also nibble hay from a box or even their litter box (they'll wisely avoid eating any hay that's been soiled).

Filling up with fresh foods

Hay certainly packs a punch in the all-important fiber department, but a rabbit must also have fresh foods (all hay and no salad makes Jack a dull rabbit).

Giving greens

Include plenty of fresh leafy greens as well as some vegetables in your rabbit's daily diet. Be aware that some rabbits, generally those on a strictly pelleted diet, may have some diarrhea or loose stools when first being fed veggies. It's best to start slowly, perhaps a small piece of carrot or bit of lettuce, to let your rabbit's system get used to them. Slowly introduce new foods, one at a time, so you can monitor your bunny's litter box for problems (see Chapter 7).

After your bunny is in a veggie sort of way, strive to feed him three different kinds of green vegetables each day. As for the amount you should feed, a good rule to follow is for every 2 pounds (.9 kilograms) of rabbit, feed 1 cup of greens (divided into the day's two meals). So, a 6-pounder (2.7-kilogram bunny) would get about 3 cups a day.

Most vegetables and greens are good for your rabbit, with some important exceptions listed in this chapter (the HRS Web site has a complete list). You can get a good start with the list below:

- Broccoli and kale (may cause gas)
- Carrot tops (the carrots themselves are pretty sugary; use as treats)

- ✔ Celery (remove stringy parts or chop into small pieces)
- ✔ Greens — beet, collard, dandelion (no chemicals, please), mustard
- ✔ Herbs — basil, cilantro, mint, parsley
- ✔ Lettuce (dark-leafed only; avoid iceberg because of high water content)
- ✔ Other "salad" greens — endive, escarole, and spinach

Whatever you do feed your bunny should be fresh, of course, well washed, and free of seeds and any rotten or spoiled areas; if possible, *organic* produce (that is, grown without the use of chemical fertilizers or pesticides) is best.

Getting fruity

Because of their high sugar and caloric content, fruits should be fed sparingly. As much as your bunny may relish a juicy strawberry fest, limit his daily intake to about 1 ounce or 1 tablespoon per 3 pounds (1.3 kilograms) of rabbit. Bananas, grapes, and raisins are exceptionally sweet and should be used only on special occasions. Other fruits play a small but tasty part of your rabbit's diet:

- ✔ Apples (no seeds, please; they're toxic)
- ✔ Berries — blueberries, raspberries, strawberries
- ✔ Melons — cantaloupe, honeydew, watermelon
- ✔ Peaches, pears, and plums
- ✔ Tomatoes (yes, tomatoes are fruit)

Growing your own

For a truly special dining experience, offer your rabbit a home-grown assortment of veggies — grown in a pot or other container or in an outdoor garden area. The food will be the freshest it can be, and your rabbit can forage and graze like a wild bunny. Any such plants should be free of chemical sprays or fertilizers.

Thinking about pellets

Discuss rabbit nutrition with any rabbit person and you'll get an earful about pelleted food. Why the fuss? Pellets are simply nuggets of grain, hay, vitamins, and minerals that have been ground together. They can be a convenient form of energy, nutrients and, typically, fiber. Unfortunately, it's just not that simple.

For years, many thought rabbits should be fed an exclusive diet of commercial pellets. Here's the catch: Pellets may be a concentrated source of nutrients, but they're also a concentrated source of calories. And just like humans, rabbits who consume too many calories tend to become overweight, like the tubby bunny in Figure 5-1. Today, more people believe that pellets are not necessary for a house rabbit who is fed a diet of grass hay and green foods (with small amounts of fruits and vegetables). Be certain to factor in your vet's opinion before making any decision or abrupt change in your rabbit's diet.

Bulging chest

Figure 5-1: Bigger is not better. Be on the lookout for full-figured rabbits.

If you do feed your rabbit pellets as a limited part of his diet, look for those based on timothy hay, not alfalfa (unless, as discussed later in this section, your bunny has special needs). Not all pellets are created equal; check the nutritional content on the package: Fiber content should be high, around 20 percent; the protein content should be lower (around 16 percent) and the fat content should be about 2 percent. Avoid any pellets mix with seeds, nuts, or dried fruits, which are fattening and can cause health problems in rabbits.

As with anything destined for your bunny's belly, the pellets you buy should be fresh (look for a manufacturing date on the bag). Only buy enough pellets for a month's supply; the following section will give you an idea of how much to serve each day. To maintain their freshness, store pellets in a cool dry place (consider an airtight storage container). Finally, toss out any pellets your rabbit doesn't eat before replacing them with new pellets.

Eating for life

What and how much you feed your rabbit will depend on a number of factors, including age, weight, and overall health. As always, consult your vet. You'll feed your rabbit twice a day, so divide the quantities of veggies in half; for example, 3 cups of greens a day equals 1½ cups at each of two meals. The following guidelines may be modified to suit your own rabbit:

- ✔ **Babies:** Up until about seven weeks, kits (baby rabbits) rely on their mother's milk for their nutrition. At four weeks or so, they can nibble and get used to alfalfa and pellets.

- ✔ **Youngsters (eight weeks to eight months):** During this time of rapid growth, provide grass hay (add a handful of alfalfa hay for an extra boost) and some pellets; *slowly* introduce veggies at 12 weeks.

- ✔ **Teenagers (eight months to one year):** Growth is beginning to slow down, so decrease pellets to about ½ cup per 6 pounds (2.7 kilograms) of rabbit weight. Continue to offer unlimited grass hay and introduce more vegetables. Introduce fruit as a treat, but limit to 1 or 2 tablespoons per 6 pounds (2.7 kilograms) of bunny.

- ✔ **Adults (one to five years):** When an adult stops growing his caloric needs decrease. Provide unlimited timothy hay; for every 2 pounds (.9 kilograms) of rabbit feed 1 cup of vegetables and ¼ to ½ cup of high-fiber pellets. Decrease pellets and increase hay and greens if weight gain becomes an issue.

- ✔ **Seniors (six years and older):** Continue a normal adult diet, unless the older rabbit has problems maintaining weight. If so, and when advised by a vet, give extra pellets and alfalfa hay.

- ✔ **Ill or recovering rabbits:** Rabbits who are ill or recovering from an injury often need extra energy and nutrients to bounce back. Additional pellets often do the trick. It's best to consult your vet before making any changes or adding supplements.

- ✔ **Rotund rabbits:** Overweight rabbits need fewer calories. Eliminate or greatly restrict pellets. Continue to offer unlimited grass hay as at least 1 cup of fresh greens per 2 pounds (.9 kilograms)of rabbit. Restrict or eliminate sweet treats (even carrots) until weight loss goals are met.

- ✔ **Mommies and Mommies-to-be:** Pregnant and nursing *does* (females) need extra calories and nutrients. Provide a good supply of fresh hay, nutritious greens, water, and pellets. Your vet can determine if additional supplements are necessary.

Treating for your sweet

Obesity is a problem with domestic rabbits; no doubt, sweet snacks play their part. If you do treat your rabbit, curb the potential for obesity by doing it only occasionally (maybe once a day or as a reward during training); by offering a bit of fresh fruit (see the list above); by avoiding commercially prepared treats (they're the rabbit equivalent of junk food); and by using some petting or play time as a fine reward for your rabbit.

Knowing food no-nos

For a number of unpleasant reasons, including gas, diarrhea, obesity, and gastrointestinal disease, you should avoid feeding a diet high in fats, starches, and sugars. More specifically, do not feed the following foods:

- Beans (any kind)
- Breads and cereals
- Chocolate
- Corn
- Grains (wheat, oats, etc.)
- Nuts and seeds
- Peas
- Potatoes
- Refined sugars

Hydrating for health

Water is a critical part of a rabbit's health, so supply yours with fresh water at all times. Whether in a water bottle or a ceramic crock, replace your rabbit's water at least once a day (and clean the bottle or crock each day). Take note of how much water your rabbit is drinking; some rabbits do better with water bottles than others. If your bunny doesn't take to the bottle, go for the bowl.

If you're caring for a rabbit out of doors, pay special attention to his water supply. Cold temperatures can freeze a water bottle into a useless chunk of ice (sound like another reason to keep your rabbit indoors?) and warm temperatures can both increase your rabbit's thirst and cause water to foul more quickly.

Keeping Fit: Sprints and High Jumps

A rabbit who doesn't get enough exercise everyday is at risk for a number of serious health problems, including obesity, poor bone density, poor muscle tone, sore *hocks* (undersides of feet), urinary infections, and gastrointestinal distress (more on these in Chapter 7). An inactive rabbit can also suffer from boredom, depression, and problematic chewing and digging.

Don't worry, your rabbit doesn't need to be on a treadmill or playing catch with you for hours at a time, but he does needs time outside of his cage or hutch. Many recommend at least two to three hours a day of exercise (others say more like five), with the understanding that much of that "exercise" consists of freedom to roam and play in a room, indoor enclosure, or secure outdoor run. Read on for fun ways to get the most out of your bunny's workouts.

Moving around indoors

If your rabbit lives in your home but spends part of his day (while you're at work or school) in his cage, he'll need some time and some space for his daily exercise session. Decide where his "gym" will be — the whole house, one room, or a penned in area — and make sure it has been carefully rabbit-proofed (Chapter 4). If you make this time part of your daily routine, you can let him out when you get home from work and he can run around until bedtime.

If you can take a break from your nightly activities, get down on the floor and play games like hide-and-seek with your rabbit; he'll also just enjoy sitting with you as your read or watch television. Try some creative tactics to keep him hopping. Set up an obstacle course of sorts using boxes, ramps, and tunnels. Or use a multi-level carpeted cat condo to get him moving. Of course, toys are always a great way to motivate play.

Taking a break outdoors

Even a rabbit kept in a large hutch needs freedom to exercise in a larger space. If you can't bring your rabbit indoors for his out time, read Chapter 4 on the ways you'll need to protect your rabbit and your yard. Safety is your primary concern, so *never* leave a rabbit outdoors unattended. A secure bunny run, with a top and four sides is a good option, but not fool-proof (rabbits can dig down and out, predators can get too close for comfort). And while the fresh air is good, you may need to motivate him with boxes for hopping in and out of, tubes for tunneling, and ramps for climbing. Don't forget a toy or two as well (see Chapter 4 for more on toys).

Wrangling Your Rabbit

When a rabbit is picked up in the wild, he's usually about to be harmed or killed by a predator. That instinct to keep his feet on the ground lives on in your domesticated bunny, and many *really* don't like to be picked up. So, when handling your bunny, it's best to do it properly and only when necessary.

It's easier to pick up a rabbit who trusts you. To achieve that trust, you both time and some patience. If you have a bunny who's new to you, you'll be starting from scratch, although young bunnies tend to be easier. To start, get down near your bunny and let him approach you (*never* chase a rabbit). A small bit of treat may entice your bunny over to your hand for some petting. Your rabbit will get increasingly comfortable with you if you spend a few minutes a day working on this. Only after your rabbit comes to you and allows you to gently stroke the top of his head should you think about lifting him.

Putting safety first

A rabbit who doesn't trust you is likely to struggle out of your grasp and injure himself. Even a rabbit who usually tolerates being handled can suddenly twist or leap out of your grip. To protect yourself from an unhappy rabbit's sharp claws, wear a long-sleeved shirt. You should never lift a rabbit by the ears or the scruff of his neck. And never hold a rabbit by his back legs — a rabbit held tightly like that can kick and break or injure his own back. A fall (or a drop) from your arms can also injure or break a rabbit's back.

Lifting with care

Your goal should be to lift your rabbit safely, in a way that makes him feel secure about being up in the air. You may modify or choose a different method of lifting and carrying, as long as it works for you and is safe for your rabbit.

1. **Kneel down. Slide one hand down the rabbit's side while petting his head with your other hand.**

2. **Slide the arm at your rabbit's side under his chest and move your petting hand down under to support his hindquarters, as in Figure 5-2.**

Figure 5-2: Get a grip! Holding your rabbit properly will help prevent injuries.

3. **Scoop him closely to you and hold firmly, not tightly.**

4. **Stand up slowly, keeping your rabbit close to you. Hug the rabbit if he starts to struggle. Don't drop him, especially from a standing position.**

5. **When it's time to put him down, do so carefully. Hold him close until you are back in a kneeling position, and then let him go on the floor.**

Most importantly, be sure to support your rabbit's hind end, and keep him from falling out of your arms. All of this will take practice. A small treat will reward your rabbit and help him relax a bit when you put him down.

Taking care with kids

Young children can spend time with rabbits, but they should always be carefully supervised. You can show a child how to pet a rabbit on the floor — gently, with the back of their hand even — and you can teach them not to pick up, chase, or harass a rabbit.

An older child, one who is at least eight years old and who is capable of proper handling, may be ready to learn how to pick up a small rabbit. Keep in mind that a frightened rabbit will bite, scratch, or kick — injuring himself and the child. Unfortunately, many rabbits suffer broken bones or become paralyzed from being accidentally dropped by children. Please use great caution!

Becoming Fluffy and Flea Free: Grooming

Rabbits take care of much of their own personal hygiene and grooming; you'll probably notice yours doing quite a bit of licking and preening. But to keep your rabbit well-groomed you need to lend a hand, mainly when it comes to coat, nail, and ear care. Keep brushes (pin and soft-bristled), a flea comb (wide-toothed for long-haired rabbits), a nail trimmer and styptic powder (or corn starch), and cotton swabs handy to make your grooming easier.

Use the time you spend grooming your rabbit to look for any lumps, signs of illness, eye discharge, teeth problems, sores, or cuts (see Chapter 7 for more on these). Make this part of your weekly schedule (an hour or less), unless yours is shedding or you have a long-haired rabbit who needs daily brushing.

Brushing for beginners

Rabbits are meticulous groomers, and they do a great job of licking, cleaning, and smoothing their fur. But as those who have house rabbits will attest, hair is always an issue (on the carpet, on the furniture, in the air, etc.) Plus, because rabbits swallow so much hair they can be prone to hairballs, especially if they don't eat enough fiber or get enough exercise.

With any rabbit, take care to brush gently, in the natural direction of the coat, and avoid the delicate skin underneath. A rabbit who is not used to being groomed may need some time before he's comfortable with the process.

Follow these brushing guidelines:

- **Short and medium coats:** Allot an hour a week for most rabbits with shorter coats. Gather your tools and find a comfortable spot to sit with your rabbit in your lap. Start with a pin brush and move down in the natural direction of the coat, continuing until most of the loose hair is removed. Go on to the flea comb, looking for fleas or signs of fleas (black specks). The comb can also be use to work out any mats that have formed. If your rabbit seems tense or upset, reassure him and offer a treat if necessary. Use a bristle brush for the final touches and a bit of shine.

✔ **Long coats:** Longhaired rabbits must be brushed every day. Because their long fine hair mats very easily, you have two choices: Do the brushing — consistently and well — or have a groomer shear your rabbit (a perfectly fine way of keeping a long coat manageable and clean). To brush, find a comfortable spot to sit with your rabbit in your lap. Start with a pin brush and brush through thin sections of your rabbit's coat, from the skin out. Matted areas can be taken out with a flea comb if possible; otherwise, they'll need to be carefully cut out with scissors or a mat rake. Continue with the wide-toothed comb and then the bristle brush, again moving through in the natural direction of the coat.

Trimming like a pro

Keep your rabbit's nails trimmed (and yourself free of painful scratches) with clippers designed for a cat's nails. Clipping can be a bit intimidating; have someone help you in the beginning. Hold your rabbit securely, perhaps in a towel, and cut only the tips of the nails — not the *quick,* or pinkish vein inside. Use styptic powder to stop any bleeding. Although they'll probably need trimming every two or so months, check their length during your weekly grooming sessions. For those with hard-to-handle bunnies, a vet can do the job.

Bathing bunnies

Rabbits do not enjoy bathing; fortunately for us and them, they rarely require it. More often, a rabbit will have an area that needs spot cleaning (usually the feet or rear end). In these cases, you can use a mild cleanser (those for cats work fine), some water, and a washcloth. In more extreme cases, you'll need to submerge the area in a shallow bath, wash, then rinse. Do not submerge the entire rabbit! Dry your bunny completely before putting him back in his cage.

Don't forget the ears!

Check your rabbit's glorious ears each week — they should be smooth and clean. Using a cotton swab you can gently remove debris or excess wax from the outer ear canal only. Take a peek for signs of ear mites (redness, dark wax, or something that looks like dirt). Talk to your vet if you feel your rabbit's ears have issues or need additional cleaning.

Chapter 6

Getting to Know Your Rabbit

• •

In This Chapter

▶ Finding your inner rabbit

▶ Taking part in bunny banter

▶ Socializing your rabbit

▶ Training 101

▶ Managing a badly behaving bunny

• •

*I*n any good relationship, communication is the key to success. You and your rabbit are no exception. Although your bunny may seem a bit quiet, she has many ways of communicating her needs. After you're better able to "speak" with your bunny, you'll be better equipped to handle any behavioral problems that may arise. Worried about biting? Have a problem nibbler? Read on.

Thinking Like a Bunny

To truly communicate with your bunny you need to understand where she is coming from. Although your domesticated bunny, which shares many of the survival traits of her wild ancestors, should never experience life as a prey animal, she instinctively behaves as though she does. So keep the following instincts in mind so you're better equipped to ease your rabbit's worries:

✔ **Fear of predators:** Your rabbit is easily frightened of predators — including humans — so don't act like one. Never chase your bunny or move quickly toward her. Handle your bunny gently, and don't hold her against her will. Also, consider the effect that your other pets may have on your bunny's nerves.

✔ **Need for being social:** In the wild, rabbits live very social lives within a group or colony. Provide your bunny with a similar living situation — secure places for safety and rest, as well as plenty of time interacting with you, other bunnies, or other pets. This will require a good deal of petting (from you) and some licking or even nipping (from your bunny).

✓ **Fear of loud noises:** Loud noises may startle some bunnies (remember that acute sense of hearing?); speak softly to your pet and be aware of loud household noises such as vacuum cleaners, screaming children, or other pets.

✓ **Need for a specific schedule:** Bunnies have their own schedule, one that's been dictated by ages of evolution. They eat, play, and explore in the morning and evening — when they are most active (and when there are fewer predators about). Respect this natural behavior — especially when your rabbit is determined to snooze all afternoon.

Speaking Rabbit

In nature, rabbits communicate with each other using sounds and body movements. As a member of your domesticated rabbit's "colony," she'll communicate with you using the same intricate language. So be sure to listen" by observing her movements, expressions, and subtle signals. Think about the context in which any cluck, twitch, or shake is given.

Interpreting bunny banter

Although you'll find that body language plays a more important role than vocalizations in the way your bunny communicates, you should be able to interpret the following sounds you hear your quiet companion utter:

✓ **Purr:** "I'm quite content." Also called a *tooth purr,* this is the sound a happy bunny makes by lightly grinding her teeth together. Loud grinding means your pet is in pain; seek veterinary help.

✓ **Hum:** "I'm in the mood for love." You're likely to hear this mainly from those male bunnies still sexually intact.

✓ **Cluck:** "My, that was delicious." A rabbit's faint clucking sound is the ultimate snack review. Keep up the good work.

✓ **Whimper:** "Please leave me alone, and definitely don't pick me up." Pregnant rabbits are most likely to use this, but others may employ it as well.

✓ **Snort or grunt:** "I'm annoyed, even angry." Stop whatever you are doing. A series of these may be followed by a bite or a lunge.

✓ **Shrill scream:** "I'm in extreme pain or dying." This sound is unmistakable, much like a human scream, and it's very serious (it can also be an indication of extreme fear). Call a veterinarian immediately.

Doing the bunny hop

Better understand your bunny by understanding the following body language:

- **Dancing, hopping, and leaping:** "I'm happy, happy, happy." Bunnies express pleasure like this with many variations and levels of difficulty.

- **Racing:** "Whoopee!" Stand back and enjoy the joyous, sometimes zigzaggy, show.

- **Binky-ing:** "It's hard to describe how happy I am!" The binky, a high jump coupled with vigorous twists, is the unmistakable sign of a very happy rabbit.

- **Flat-out stretching:** "Ah, What a life. . . ." A rabbit completely at ease will rest on her stomach with her legs stretched out behind her. Only a "flop," when a rabbit sprawls on her side or back, is better.

- **Presenting:** "How 'bout some grooming?" Your rabbit is looking for a scratch when she lowers her head to the floor, with hindquarters slightly raised

- **Licking:** "I'm actually quite fond of you." You are loved when your rabbit licks you; gentle nibbling may indicate the same.

- **Circling your feet:** "I'm in the mood for love." This sign of courting behavior may also be used just to get your attention.

- **Chinning:** "This is mine; so is this." By rubbing her chin on an object (or your hand) a male marks her turf using scent from glands under her chin. Fortunately, the odor can't be detected by humans.

- **Sitting up tall:** "I'm curious," or "Hey, is there trouble afoot?" An inquisitive rabbit will rear up on her hind end to look around. A frightened rabbit, however, may rear up and prepare to bite.

- **Head butting:** "Hey!" or "Gimme some of that." A persistent rabbit will head-butt you when she wants something — food, petting, whatever. This is usually very cute.

- **Biting:** "No, no way." A bite is not the same as a nip, and you'll know the difference when you get your first real chomp. A little nip can mean, "Hey," or "move over"; a bite is usually delivered by an angry or fearful rabbit.

- **Kicking:** "Let go!" or "Wow! What fun!" A rabbit will use a wicked high back kick when she's being held the wrong way. The other kind — of the joyful, playful variety — is usually out to the side.

✔ **Thumping:** "Warning!" or, maybe, "I'm annoyed." Stomping her hind legs on the ground is a rabbit's way of alerting you to danger or to something else that's going on.

The ears have it

Whether lop or not, bunny ears play an important part in a rabbit's body language. For bunnies with upright ears, the signals are pretty clear, but lop-eared movements are much more subtle; watch carefully for the following:

✔ **Facing forward and pointing up** indicates that "everything's fine." When ears are facing forward and tilting forward, a bunny's curiosity is aroused. A variation of this: ears stretched out like television antennae.

✔ **When the ears begin to turn away from you and/or go back a bit** indicates that you have an unhappy bunny on your hands. The farther the ears go back, the worse things are. One ear up and one ear down is a more mildly unhappy rabbit.

✔ **Ears pulled tightly back,** combined with a flattened body and bulging eyes, clearly indicates fear. Don't confuse flattening with a more relaxed version, the squat, which is a sign of a bunny at ease.

✔ **Shaking her ears from side to side** is her way of telling you she's had enough, whether it's petting, food, or otherwise. Look at the intensity of the shake — was that a polite "No, thanks," or a "Get that yucky snack away from me!"?

The nose knows

A bunny's nose is the most important way she senses the world. Your rabbit's nose wiggles to some degree most of the time, although it's not necessarily to smell things. Often, a wiggle of your rabbit's nose indicates the following moods or interests:

✔ **Wiggling nose:** When your bunny's calm, her nose wiggles fairly slowly and evenly. Wiggle speed increases as your bunny becomes more agitated or interested in something.

✔ **Nudging nose:** Your bunny may also use her nose for nudging — as a casual greeting, a gentle (or firm) appeal for petting, or a request to move out of the way. Nose-to-nose nuzzling can often replace licking as a show of affection.

Noticing tell-tail signs

A bunny uses her fluffy white tail to warn her companions of danger in the wild. In your home, your pet may not have a lot to say about hawks and foxes, but her cotton tail still holds a wealth of the following wisdom:

- **A tail that's down, with just a bit of white showing,** means your bunny is relaxed.

- **A tall raised tail** can mean that your bunny is agitated or excited about a toy or delicious treat, a potential conflict, an approaching lover.

- **A twitching tail** may indicate courting or competing rabbits.

- **A vigorous twitch with a turnaround** means "No, thanks!" or "As if!!"

- **A bunny-butt-in-the-face is,** simply, backtalk

Introducing Other Pets

Unless she lives in a colony, a rabbit yearns for some company. Aside from mating (not a concern for most pet rabbits, which should be spayed and neutered), you should be able to provide most of the love and respect your own rabbit needs. Still, you may be tempted to find a live-in friend for your bunny, or, perhaps, introduce her to a pet you already have.

Not just any creature combination will do for your bunny. Just like rabbits in the wild, domesticated rabbits follow a hierarchical system with dominant and submissive members. For a successful rabbit-to-rabbit pairing, look for complimentary personalities; two aggressive rabbits may not live happily ever after, but two docile ones could. Typically, two female rabbits fare pretty well together, but be prepared for two male rabbits to clash.

If you're a natural-born pet lover, there's a good chance you're already living with one — a cat, dog, guinea pig, bird, etc. Consider your bunny's fear of predators when pairing her with any other kind of pet. Remember, your ultimate goal is to make your jittery little bunny feel relaxed and safe in her home. If your rabbit feels as though she is being stalked or hunted, she will let you know. Take the following precautions with the animals listed below to ensure that your bunny and potential buddy play it safe:

- ✔ **Cats:** Your kitty may not be particularly aggressive or able to harm your rabbit, but cats are predators by nature. You can test the cohabitation waters by carefully introducing the two, but pay close attention to each animal's behavior. If your cat is stalking or looks interested in a chase, consider a leash or harness for her, at least in the beginning. On the other hand, your rabbit may be bigger — or tougher — than your cat, and you'll have to protect kitty from a formidable bunny stomp. For safety, keep both of their nails trimmed short.

- ✔ **Dogs:** For many dogs, there's nothing better than a good old-fashioned chase — squirrel, cat, rabbit, it doesn't matter. Does this mean that dogs and rabbits can't live together in harmony? Certainly not. It does mean that you should carefully evaluate a dog's personality before you consider such an arrangement. Certain types of dogs — some terriers and hounds — have hunting bred right into them. Even if your old dog hasn't hunted in years, the sight of your new little bunny hopping down the hallway could bring back some strong memories. If you feel that your pooch may be a good bunny mate, play it safe. Try a short meeting with the dog leashed and the rabbit in her cage. Continue this until both animals seem at ease. Even after this, however, they should never be left alone. Please note that puppies (regardless of breed) are the worst kind of dog to pair up with a rabbit; their playfulness can lead to death in a rabbit.

- ✔ **Other pets:** When considering any other pets, take a moment to think about the same pairing in the wild. Could your canary take on your bunny? If not, then they'll probably do fine when supervised at home. Same for guinea pigs, hamsters, etc. Ferrets are serious rabbit predators and should be kept away from your bunny.

Your animals may get along splendidly, which is wonderful. Done properly, life indoors can even ease your little bunny's fears of being eaten for lunch. But don't let down your guard. Carefully supervising contact between your animals may prevent tragic consequences.

Sit! Stay! Hop! Training Your Rabbit

Whether you have a behavioral problem to deal with, a litter box you hope will be used, or you'd just like to have some fun with your rabbit, training can be very rewarding. It helps to have a good understanding of how a rabbit communicates, fits into a social structure, and reacts to natural rabbit urges such as digging, all of which is covered in this book's first chapter.

You are bound to encounter some behavioral problems with your rabbit, whether she's chewing, biting, soiling, or a little bit of everything. Faced with these bumps in the road, most people feel frustrated, angry, or, worse, they feel like giving up. Don't give up! Although annoying at times, most of these situations have solutions (keep reading!).

Before you take on your troublemaker or think about bunny tricks, take a few minutes to check out these helpful training principles and guidelines.

Being a great trainer

No matter how bright your bunny is, she is not going to get very far training herself. This is where you come in — the trainer extraordinaire! As with many other companion animals, real training success depends on a great trainer.

Before you begin any kind of training you should have already established a good bond with your rabbit; in other words, your rabbit must trust you before she will be able to listen to you. After you've reached this point, you can think about what you'd like to focus on — litter box, chewing, coming when called, or other "tricks."

Use the following tips to make training more productive:

- **Be smart:** Your trainee learns best in the proper environment. Choose a small, quiet room where you won't be interrupted by other humans or pets (a laundry room or bathroom, perhaps). Bunny-proof the room before you get started (see Chapter 4). Keep your training sessions short, 10 to 15 minutes at the most.

- **Be consistent:** Use the same command — going from "come!" to "okay, come here!" only confuses your student. Be patient and keep in mind that your rabbit doesn't know your language, and she's not sure why you want her to do these silly things over and over. End each session on a high note, before she gets tired or frustrated. Stick with it — a bit every day — success doesn't happen overnight.

- **Be the boss:** Be firm, but not harsh. Saying "No!" is often enough to stop a rabbit from what she's doing; the key is to quickly redirect your bunny's attention elsewhere. If you find your rabbit digging up a corner of your carpet, say "No!" and then give her a box of papers or an old piece of carpeting to go at.

Never use physical discipline with a rabbit — they are too fragile, and it only destroys the trust that you've worked so hard at. On the other hand, just because you're being firm with your corrections doesn't mean you can't reward your student for good behavior with a nutritious treat or some petting.

The poop on housetraining

For many, the most important part of training is the litter box, especially for rabbits who live indoors with free rein of the house or part of it (it also makes it easier to clean up after any rabbit). Most rabbits take to a litter box fairly quickly because of their natural desire to keep their living quarters clean; they'll usually pick one "toilet" spot and stick to it. Your job is to find out where your rabbit will best use a litter box, then to encourage her to do so. As with any training endeavor, patience and consistency are key. Also, a spayed or neutered rabbit is far less likely to spray or mark territory, which will make housetraining possible. Follow these steps down the road to success:

1. **Keep your rabbit in her cage:** Set up a litter box with litter (see Chapter 4), preferably in a corner. Because many rabbits like to poop while eating, a bit of hay may encourage her to hop in and stick around to take care of business.

2. **Watch to see that your rabbit is using the box:** Move it if she seems to prefer another area of the cage. Praise her and continue until she has the hang of it.

3. **Let her out into a small area under close supervision after you have success in the cage:** Pop her back into her litter box every now and then to remind her how it's done. And set up another litter box (add some poops or wet litter to make is smell homey) in case she can't make it back into the cage in time to use her primary box.

4. **Herd her quickly over to a litter box when you see her back up with her tail lifted slightly or if you catch her in the act:** Don't scold or punish.

5. **Expand your rabbit's boundaries, her time out of the cage, and the number of times she's out each day gradually:** Add litter boxes as you need them, watching her and moving the box if she prefers another area.

6. **Remember that she *will* have accidents — that's okay:**
A new rabbit needs to mark her territory with some pellets
in the beginning. Clean up with a commercial pet odor
remover or diluted white vinegar (to keep her from using
that spot again). Go back a few steps if your rabbit ever
seems to need a refresher course.

When Good Bunnies are Bad

Earlier in this chapter you can read about the natural instincts and
urges that are part of being a bunny as well as some thoughts on
training. But you can tackle these problems before they become
serious. Even better, you can prevent them from becoming a problem in the first place.

Chew this

As good as chewing is for your rabbit and her teeth, all that chomp-
ing creates a lot of concern for those who share their homes — and
their furniture, rugs, books, shoes — with a rabbit. After you've
done your rabbit-proofing (refer to Chapter 4), you can concentrate
on redirecting your rabbit's chewing urges. Whenever you see your
bunny start to nibble on a forbidden item, quickly give her something
else to chew, preferably something similar in taste and texture. Some
people find that saying "no" or clapping their hands when they see
the "bad" behavior can help.

Marking turf

It's one of the more unpleasant rabbit behaviors out there —
territorial urination. It may seem like your rabbit is peeing on your
walls, furniture, and carpeting, but she's really just telling you and
any other rabbits that this is her territory. Intact males and females
both dabble in spraying, though males do so more commonly and
aggressively. Because bunnies are hormonally motivated, the first
thing you should do is spay or neuter your rabbit. You should also
consider any circumstances surrounding the pee incident.

Ouch! Battling a biter

A rabbit will bite for a number of very valid rabbit reasons, none of
which will be very comforting if you happen to be the recipient of
a well-directed bite. Think about what's going on in your bunny's

head — it's unlikely that she's just being mean and nasty. Look at the following common biting scenarios to see if yours fits in somewhere or makes more sense:

- **Food for thought:** Many caretakers report being bitten when they bring their rabbit her food. Not nice! In your rabbit's mind, she's feeling very protective of her bowl, and she wants to be certain you won't carry it away. Hand feeding may help to associate your hand (a good thing) with food.

- **Fear factor:** A nip may mean "You scare me when you reach into my cage" or "I don't trust you to pick me up." With this type of fearful biting, you should go back and work more on trust and handling (Chapter 5). Because a rabbit has a blind spot directly in front of her face, you'll be less likely to frighten yours if you approach her from the side.

- **Bully bunnies:** If you're getting nipped throughout the day, for sitting on the sofa or walking through a room, your rabbit is probably showing you that she's the boss (or so she thinks!). Show her that you are the dominant "bunny." Letting out a loud and sudden screech when bitten can send her the message that this type of bullying is not allowed.

- **All out of love:** Intact rabbits may also bite, just out of feeling sexually frustrated. The solution is simple: spay or neuter your rabbit to reduce many aggressive behaviors, including biting, circling, and mounting.

Kicking the habit

Like biting, kicking serves a purpose in a rabbit's mind, but that doesn't make it any easier when it's you getting beat up by a pair of strong hind legs. When she's being carried, a kick is your rabbit's way of saying "I'm outta here!" Support her properly, especially her back end, and never let her kick her way out of your arms — she's likely to be injured in the fall.

Terrible teenagers

Just like their human counterparts, adolescent rabbits (up until they are a year old) go through a "difficult" period. Though both human and rabbit teenagers partake in their fair share of high-energy antics and mischief, rabbits throw in some excessive chewing and digging for an extra challenge. You'll need to summon up a bunch of patience as your rabbit outgrows this stage (she really will!). You'll also need to step up your rabbit-proofing efforts (see Chapter 4) and engage your youngster with plenty of activities, toys, and attention.

Chapter 7

Keeping Your Rabbit Healthy

· ·

· ·

*J*ust like any other animal companion, rabbits sometimes get sick. Your rabbit is certainly going to be less prone to illness if you give him a proper diet, a clean home, and plenty of exercise — all of which is covered in this book.

Unfortunately for our furry friends, even the best cared for rabbits can contract diseases, get infections, and become injured in accidents. When it happens, you need to know what to do and who to call for help. One of the most important things you can do is to find a qualified rabbit veterinarian and establish a good relationship with him.

Finding Your Best Vet

It may be harder than you think to find a vet for your rabbit. First of all, not just any veterinarian will do. A vet who treats cats and dogs may not know enough about rabbits to care for yours. A vet that treats *exotics* (rabbits, snakes, birds) is a better bet, providing he has enough experience with rabbits. You can find such vets by the following methods:

   ✔ **Rescue groups or shelters:** If you've adopted a rabbit from a rescue group or shelter, they may refer you to someone, perhaps the same vet that has been treating your rabbit while he waited for a new home. The House Rabbit Society provides an online vet locator system (see Chapter 8).

If you still can't find a vet, look for a guinea pig or rat rescue group or club (start with the Internet); they can often refer you to a guinea pig or rat vet who also treats rabbits.

- **Referrals:** Other rabbit people can refer you to their vets or vets that they have heard good things about. Talk to as many people as you can about their experiences. One person's opinion may not be enough.

- **Club members:** Breeders or members of rabbit breed clubs can be a good source of information. You may also have luck with those involved in 4-H rabbit projects. Again, get as many recommendations as you can.

- **Veterinarians:** Vets, even if they don't treat rabbits themselves, often know of exotic vets that do. Talk to local vets or find one through a state association of veterinarians (do a search for one on the Internet).

Conducting an "interview"

After you've found a vet (or two or three) who specializes in rabbits, you need to decide whether this is the right vet for you and your rabbit (some people even like to have a backup vet, just in case). Take a few minutes to call the office and ask these important questions:

- **Do you treat house rabbits? For how long?** A vet that treats stock or show rabbits may not necessarily understand the needs of house rabbits. It's best to find someone with at least two years of experience.

- **Do you have special training in rabbit care?** Courses or conferences on rabbit health will keep a vet up to date on the latest treatment options.

- **Do you know which antibiotics are dangerous for rabbits?** A rabbit-savvy vet should know that oral amoxicillin and some other "cillin" drugs are dangerous.

- **Do you perform rabbit spays and neuters?** A vet should know the proper anesthesia procedure for rabbits (the House Rabbit Society Web site lists what's safe and what's not). Even if your rabbit is spayed or neutered, they may need surgery down the line.

- **How do you handle after-hour emergencies?** If your vet refers calls after regular business hours to another vet or clinic, you'll need to find out if this facility is equally qualified to care for your rabbit.

Going for initial and annual exams

Your vet uses an initial exam as a baseline for future exams. So it's very important to schedule an office visit as soon as you can with the vet you've chosen (never wait until you have a health crisis). This is your opportunity to look around, meet the staff, and make sure you're comfortable with your decision. Take note of the facility's general cleanliness, as well as how smoothly things seem to be running. This is also a good time to ask about the vet's fees.

During this initial exam you get to meet the vet and see how she handles your rabbit. This is your vet's chance to get to know your rabbit and talk to you about his general health and any guidelines (like his diet) that she'd like you to try. This is also a good time to talk about spaying or neutering (if you haven't done so already).

After the initial exam, your vet should examine your rabbit once a year, whether he needs it or not. During an annual checkup, a vet will check your rabbit from head to toe, looking for any changes or signs of trouble. This is also the time to take care of nail clipping, ear cleaning, or teeth trimming that may be required. Unlike dogs, rabbits in the United States don't need vaccinations.

No Fooling Around: *Spay and Neuter*

You should spay or neuter your rabbit (if you're thinking about breeding, see Chapter 2 for the many reasons why most people shouldn't). Spaying and neutering helps with behavior problems, housetraining, unwanted bunnies, and it is a great way to improve your rabbit's health.

For a female rabbit, *spaying* (having her uterus and ovaries removed) virtually eliminates the risk of reproductive cancers. Females can be safely spayed at about six months, but it's best to do it before she reaches the age of two, when uterine and ovarian cancers can begin to strike. If you've adopted an older rabbit, have your vet do a blood panel before scheduling surgery, to make sure there won't be any problems.

For a male rabbit, *neutering* (having his testicles removed) reduces or eliminates annoying territorial spraying and aggression. His health should improve because he's less likely to be injured in battles with rabbits and other pets. Males can be safely neutered at four months.

In the right hands, these procedures are safe and relatively simple, but they do involve anesthesia; be certain to find a vet who has experience altering *rabbits* (not just cats or dogs).

Preventing and Detecting Illness

The best way of dealing with a health problem is to prevent it from happening in the first place. With a rabbit, this means a healthy diet with lots of plant fiber, a clean home (preferably indoors), daily doses of exercise, low-stress living conditions, and proper handling (more on all these topics can be found in Chapter 5). Rabbits hide their symptoms well when they do get sick. So you need to know what your bunny's body feels and looks like when he's healthy, so you can spot any subtle changes that may indicate a problem.

In addition to visiting the vet annually, daily, you should sit with your rabbit, hold him, and pet him. While you're hanging out together, do the following five-point check:

1. **Check his eyes:** They should be clear, clean, and free of discharge.

2. **Check his ears:** They should be clean and smooth, without sores or flaking.

3. **Check his teeth:** They should be aligned and not broken.

4. **Pet his fur**: Feel his body for unusual lumps, bruises, cuts, or sores.

5. **Peek at his privates:** The area should be clean and dry (see Chapter 5 to find how to clean the area if it isn't).

It may not be much fun, but it's important to get to know what's coming out of your rabbit. Changes in urine and feces can signal serious health problems. Do the following every day:

- ✔ **Check your rabbit's urine for unusual color, odor, or consistency.** Changes in urine or urination habits may be a sign of dietary changes or disease (see later in this chapter).

- ✔ **Check your rabbit's droppings and get an idea of what's normal.** Any changes in size and consistency can indicate a gastrointestinal problem (see later in this chapter).

Being Aware of Health Hazards

Because rabbits don't always stay healthy from one annual visit to another, I've provided an overview of health problems you may be faced with and how best to handle them. Some of these concerns are more common than others, and if you are ever in question about your rabbit's health, call your vet right away. In many cases, waiting too long to get help can have disastrous results.

Certain antibiotics do more harm than good when it comes to rabbits. Oral penicillins, such as amoxicillin, for example, have been known to cause enteritis and even lead to death (See "Enteritis and enterotoxaemia" in this chapter). Some antibiotics are safe, however, and can be given orally, topically, or by injection. A rabbit-savvy vet will be aware of what's safe and what's not.

GI bunny: Gastrointestinal issues

Problems in a rabbit's sensitive digestive system may signal other medical concerns or be the result of an improper diet. Either way, it's a good idea to understand how this specialized gastrointestinal (GI) tract works and what foods it needs to stay healthy, so read all about it in Chapter 5 if you haven't already done so.

Abnormal droppings

Many companion rabbits suffer from what is known as *intermittent soft stools*. These rabbits produce soft or pudding-like droppings instead of their normal cecotropes (see Chapter 5 for an explanation of cecotropes and why rabbits usually eat them). These soft stools, which appear with normal dry droppings, stick to a rabbit's hind end causing irritation and a foul odor, as well as a terrible mess for caretakers. This condition is most commonly caused by a diet that is too low in fiber and/or too high in carbohydrates (obesity may also be a factor). In most cases, a vet will conduct some tests and then recommend a diet of grass hay and greens with no commercial foods.

Diarrhea, when there are no formed droppings and the feces is watery, is very different from soft stools. True diarrhea is rare in rabbits, and it is often a sign of a more serious or even fatal condition. Consider it an emergency and call your vet.

Stasis and obstruction

In a digestive system with normal *motility* (movement), whatever a rabbit eats moves quickly and efficiently through and out of the GI tract. One of the main components of such a healthy system is a diet high in plant fibers and low in carbohydrates and fats. A condition called *gastrointestinal stasis* occurs when this movement is slowed and ingested material (including the hair that is naturally swallowed while grooming) becomes impacted and causes a blockage.

Signs of stasis include a gradual decrease in appetite as well as in the size of droppings (eventually a rabbit may stop eating and defecating altogether); affected rabbits may appear active and alert in the beginning, but will gradually fail. Contact your veterinarian when you first notice symptoms; stasis can typically be treated with fluids, medication, and proper diet.

When a rabbit *suddenly* stops eating, producing stools or appears to be in pain, the intestine may be completely blocked by an *obstruction*. This is a potentially deadly situation that requires immediate veterinary attention.

Enteritis and enterotoxemia

Enteritis, an inflammation or infection of the intestines, occurs when the natural bacterial balance of a rabbit's GI tract is upset and disease-causing bacteria take over. In many cases, enteritis is caused by an improper diet (not enough fiber and too many carbohydrates), but stress and certain antibiotics (See this chapter's "Bad Bunny Meds") can also play a part. Symptoms may vary, but contact your vet if you notice abnormal droppings or diarrhea, loss of appetite, lethargy, weight loss, or abdominal pain. In severe cases of enteritis, rabbits can develop enterotoxemia, a type of blood poisoning that can be fatal, especially in young rabbits.

Infectious diseases

Be on the lookout for the following infectious diseases — better yet, check out the following list so you can prevent these diseases from infecting your bunny:

> ✔ **Pasteurellosis:** What appears to be a cold in a rabbit may actually be a bacterial disease called *pasteurellosis* (the bacteria that causes the disease is commonly found in rabbits, but it may only manifest when a rabbit is stressed). A rabbit with pasteurellosis may have symptoms such as sneezing, coughing, runny nose (check for matted fur on the front legs from

attempts to wipe discharge away from nose), and difficulty breathing. Pasteurellosis is contagious, so quickly call your vet, who should test the rabbit before giving antibiotics

✔ **Myxomatosis:** *Myxomatosis* is a virus that was used in the 1800s to kill off large numbers of rabbits in Europe. Although the disease is still deadly in Europe, in the United States it is seen primarily in coastal areas of Oregon and California during summer months. Carried by wild rabbits and spread by insects, the virus causes symptoms such as lethargy, fever, and red, swollen eyelids and genitals. The best prevention is to keep your rabbits indoors. See your vet right away if you suspect myxomatosis.

✔ **Viral Hemorrhagic Disease:** Relatively few cases of *Viral Hemorrhagic Disease* (VHD) have been diagnosed in the United, but it is a deadly and infectious disease causing a lot of concern. VHD attacks the internal organs of domestic rabbits; most die within days of exposure due to hemorrhaging. Symptoms include fever, muscle spasms, and bleeding from the mouth or rectum. There is no cure, but the U.S. Department of Agriculture is carefully monitoring the disease to prevent its spread, so notify your vet as soon as you notice symptoms. As with other infectious diseases, you can better protect your rabbit by limiting his — and your — contact with other rabbits at shows or events.

✔ **Ringworm:** Although *ringworm* (not a worm but a *fungal infection*) is relatively uncommon in rabbits, it is highly contagious and can be passed between animals and humans. Look for round, hairless patches (often on the head and legs) and dry, scaly skin. A vet will usually prescribe antifungal topical and oral medications.

Urinary Tract Concerns

If you're doing a good job of keeping track of what comes out of your bunny, you may notice changes in the consistency, color, and even odor of your rabbit's urine. In some cases, these changes may be signs of trouble brewing in your rabbit's urinary tract or elsewhere.

✔ **Colored urine:** Rabbit urine comes in a variety of colors — clear, yellow, brown, rusty red, orange — and it can change for a number of reasons, including medication, stress, or change in diet. Bloody urine, which may be streaked with vivid red, can be a symptom of a bladder infection, urinary stones or, in unspayed females, uterine cancer. When in doubt, call your vet.

✔ **Urinary tract infection:** If your rabbit seems to be straining to urinate, urinating inappropriately, or using the litter box frequently but only producing a drop or two at a time (urine may also have a strong smell), he may have a urinary tract infection, or *cystitis.* Consider it an emergency if your rabbit isn't urinating at all. Such infections can be treated with antibiotics and are best prevented with plenty of water, exercise, and a clean litter box.

✔ **Kidney disease:** Some of the more common causes of kidney disease include old age, cancer, parasites (especially *E.cuniculi*), and bacterial infections. If your rabbit shows signs of increased urination and thirst, along with weight loss, depression, or poor appetite, he is likely suffering from some level of kidney malfunction and needs immediate veterinary attention.

✔ **Bladder stones and sludge:** Because rabbits excrete excess calcium through their kidneys, it is not unusual for their urine to be cloudy. However, large numbers of very fine crystals form when calcium builds up in the bladder, causing urine to be thick (like toothpaste), white, and difficult to pass — a condition known as *sludge.* Other times, this waste passes in the form of *bladder stones.* Factors that may lead to sludge or stones include genetics, obesity, a diet too high in calcium (caused by alfalfa hay and certain vegetables), and insufficient water intake. These conditions require veterinary care (stones usually require surgery); you can help prevent the problems by increasing his water intake, feeding a correct diet, and encouraging exercise.

Fleas and flies and mites! Oh, my!

Rabbits can fall prey to both internal and external parasites and pests. At best, these buggers are annoying; at worst, deadly. When grooming and handling your rabbit, check him daily and all over for signs of these uninvited guests.

✔ **Fleas:** Rabbits can get fleas just like (and sometimes *from*) cats and dogs. Use a flea comb to look for fleas themselves or dark-colored specks of *flea dirt* (feces). If possible, keep your rabbit flea-free using the comb method; otherwise, a vet may need to recommend a flea product (do not use flea remedies sold for cats and dogs!).

✔ **Flies:** Outdoor rabbits can fall victim to flies and their nasty habit of laying eggs on a rabbit's soiled rectal area. Even worse, the fly maggots burrow in and feed on a rabbit's flesh.

Your best defense: Keep your rabbit inside. Otherwise, keep his cage clean and his hind end clean and dry. Call a vet if you see irritated skin or signs of flies.

✔ **Mites:** Two types of mites cause trouble for rabbits: ear mites and fur mites. Ear mites cause itching and head-shaking (look for a dark crust or discharge in the ears). Fur mites cause patches of red, itchy, flaky skin and hair loss, sometimes in clumps. Both mites are contagious and must be treated by a vet.

✔ **Worms:** Tapeworms and pinworms are two of the parasites that can infest a rabbit. Symptoms include weight loss or a distended abdomen; you may see worms in the litter box or on your rabbit's hind end. To avoid worms keep your rabbit away from areas where other animals have defecated. Seek treatment.

✔ **Encephalitozoonosis:** *Encephalitozoon cuniculi* is a protozoan parasite that can cause severe illness in rabbits. It attacks the brain, liver, and kidneys and can cause head tilt, loss of function in the legs, and loss of balance. The parasite can be present in a rabbit's body without visible symptoms. A vet can perform tests that may lead to a diagnosis, but although some vets are using drugs for treatment, there is currently no cure.

✔ **Coccidiosis:** Coccidia are protozoan parasites that affect the intestinal tract and liver of rabbits They are commonly found in rabbits, but only rarely cause disease (more so in young rabbits). Symptoms of intestinal coccidiosis can include weight loss, soft stool, and dehydration. Coccidia can be spread through feces or through soiled food or bedding. Call a vet for treatment.

✔ **Baylisascaris:** Outdoor rabbits can be exposed to *Baylisascaris procyonis*, a roundworm transmitted through raccoon feces. Rabbits who come in contact with the feces can ingest the eggs, which hatch and migrate to a rabbit's organs. Lethargy, paralysis, head tilt, and even death may result. Prevent this serious disease by keeping a rabbit away from any areas visited by raccoons.

Heatstroke

Rabbits cannot tolerate temperatures above 80 degrees Fahrenheit (27 degrees Celsius) and they're quite susceptible to heatstroke, a dangerous and even deadly situation. Consider it an emergency if your rabbit is overheated and lethargic, panting, breathing rapidly, foaming at the mouth, or sprawled out on the floor. Call your vet right away and try to lower your rabbit's body temperature: Move him to a cooler spot and out of the sun, dampen his ears with cool water, and offer him a drink.

To prevent heatstroke, watch your rabbit very carefully on hot days (humidity makes things even worse). Keep him in the shade and make sure he has lots of fresh water. A frozen soda bottle or milk jug of water placed in the cage can help cool things down a bit as can some time indoors in air conditioning.

Dental woes

A rabbit's teeth grow continuously to keep up with all the chewing involved in grazing on grasses and plant fibers. Unfortunately, those teeth continue to grow even when a rabbit is not grazing away his days, as can happen when a companion rabbit is not fed a proper diet.

Malocclusion, a condition where a rabbit's teeth do not align but continue to grow, is the most common dental problem in companion rabbits. Because the teeth do not line up properly, they are not worn down evenly. The most obvious cases occur with a bunny's front teeth, as shown in Figure 7-1, but it can happen elsewhere.

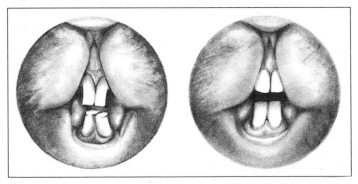

Figure 7-1: The rabbit on the left suffers from malocclusion. The rabbit on the right has excellent choppers.

If you notice that your rabbit is avoiding hard foods such as carrots, is losing weight or drooling, schedule a dental exam as soon as possible. Depending on the degree of misalignment, your rabbit's teeth may need to be trimmed regularly. Malocclusion can be hereditary or the result of an injury or poor diet.

Head tilt

Head tilt, also known as *wry neck,* is not a disease itself but a symptom of other medical problems. Although it's often caused by an ear
infection, head tilt can also be the result of encephalitozoonosis,
cancer, head trauma, or some other neurological damage. A rabbit
who is twisting his head to one side may also lose his balance or
fall over. Call a vet right away; the sooner a vet can diagnose the
cause of the head tilt the better the chance for recovery.

Obesity

Tubby bunnies are at risk for a number of health problems, including GI stasis problems, sore hocks, and urinary tract infections.
Excess weight also causes extra work for the heart and can lead to
arthritis in later years. Figure 5-1 in Chapter 5 shows what to look
for in an overweight rabbit; your vet can also tell you how much
your bunny should weigh. The "cure" for obesity is twofold: daily
exercise and a healthy diet of grass hay and fresh foods (avoid
pellets as well as starchy and sugary foods).

Sore hocks

Pododermatitis, or *sore hocks,* is a condition where the undersides
of a rabbit's feet becomes inflamed, often in conjunction with hair
loss and sores. A rabbit who is overweight, confined to a small,
damp cage, or whose feet are in constant contact with wire or hard
flooring is especially susceptible. See a veterinarian for treatment
with an antibiotic.

Aging Issues

Thanks to improved care and better living conditions, house rabbits can live 10 years or more. However, with old age comes more
health problems. Geriatric rabbits (those six years and older) may
lose a little weight and slow down a bit; arthritis, especially in the
hind legs, may make it more difficult to get around. Kidney disease,
blindness, and cancer also take their toll on senior rabbits.

A healthy diet and some special considerations will help your
rabbit cope with these changes. Lower his hay rack so it's easier to
reach. Give him a soft blanket or pad to sit on. Cut down one side
of his litter box so he can get in easier. Make his life as stress-free
as possible.

Knowing When to Call the Vet

If you're unsure whether your bunny needs vet care, use the following telltale signs as a cue that you need to call a vet:

- ✔ Lethargy or depression
- ✔ Limping or moving with effort
- ✔ Bloated tummy
- ✔ Sitting in an abnormal hunched position
- ✔ Labored or shallow breathing
- ✔ Eating or drinking less than normal
- ✔ Loud tooth grinding
- ✔ Constipation or diarrhea
- ✔ Irritability or unusual aggression
- ✔ Straining or crying when using litter box
- ✔ Discharge from the eyes, ears, or nose

Playing Doctor

Although many of the ailments described in this chapter require a veterinarian's care, it's a good idea to have some basic medical supplies on hand in case your rabbit needs minor medical attention. Grab a tool or tackle box, tape your vet's phone number and address (along with that of your backup vet) to the inside of it, and keep it in a handy location, stocked with the following:

- ✔ Antibiotic cream (for animals)
- ✔ Thermometer (animal or pediatric rectal)
- ✔ Hydrogen peroxide for cleansing
- ✔ Cotton swabs and cotton balls
- ✔ Tweezers
- ✔ Heating pad or hot water bottle for shock or hypothermia
- ✔ Styptic powder or cornstarch for bleeding nails
- ✔ Gauze bandages and sterile cotton pads for bleeding wounds
- ✔ Scissors
- ✔ Towel

Ten Must-Dos for Your Rabbit

When you care for a bunny, you can't skip over anything or promise to "do it tomorrow." When you neglect your rabbit, she suffers. So do the following and do the right thing.

✔ **Feed her the best, freshest foods you can.**
Feed your rabbit a healthy diet of fresh grass hay and greens. Commercial pellets can't take the place of a hay rack full of sweet-smelling timothy hay with an ample side dish of crisp romaine, mustard greens, and parsley.

✔ **Change her water every day.**
Dump that bowl or bottle, clean it, and refill it with fresh water everyday.

✔ **Don't forget her out time and exercise.**
She needs plenty of exercise and time out of her cage. Your rabbit needs at least two to four hours (more is better) of time to hop, run, and play.

✔ **Take a peek at her poop for problems.**
It may not be pretty, but your rabbit's waste droppings can tell you a lot about what's going on with her health.

✔ **Find a good vet and schedule an annual checkup.**
Don't wait until you have a medical emergency to find a veterinarian for your rabbit. Your rabbit needs a checkup at least once a year.

✔ **Check her often for health problems.**
Make it a part of your daily routine to handle your rabbit and check for any unusual discharge, lumps, sores, or skin problems.

✔ **Observe her body language and "listen" to what she has to say.**
Listen to any clucks, whimpers, and snorts very carefully. Watch her body language for subtle messages.

✔ **Clean up! Get serious once a week about cage cleanliness.**
In addition to your daily cleaning routine, thoroughly clean and disinfect your rabbit's cage and accessories once a week to keep her in good health.

✔ **Keep up with grooming — weekly (daily, if necessary).**
Weekly, you should brush out loose hair (daily for long hair), check and trim nails, and check ears for mites or wax buildup.

✔ **Spend some quality time with her.**
Your rabbit craves a social life; so, get down on the floor and play with her or have her sit next to you while you read or talk on the phone.

Ten Resources for Parents of Rabbits

Check out the following selection of resources for guidance in your own bunny endeavors.

✔ www.petfinder.com
   Search for adoptable pets in your area, use the resource library with information about rabbit care, and scan the lost and found classifieds.

✔ **The House Rabbit Society (HRS)**
   HRS is an invaluable source of information on adoption, health care, behavior, diet, litter-box training, and more (510/970-7575; www.rabbit.org).

✔ www.veterinarypartner.com
   This site features loads of articles, up-to-date health information, and a library of rabbit info.

✔ **House Rabbit Network**
   This group (www.rabbitnetwork.org) is dedicated to rescuing and finding indoor homes for rabbits and educating the public.

✔ **Oxbow Pet Products**
   If you're looking for quality foods for your rabbit, order from the Web site, www.oxbowhay.com or contact Oxbow at (800) 249-0366.

✔ **Rabbit magazines and publications**
   Check out *Rabbits Only* (516/737-0763; www.rabbits.com) and *Rabbits U.S.A.* or *Critters* (949/855-8822; www.animal network.com).

✔ **Pet Sitters**
   Check out the National Association of Pet Sitters (856/439-0324; www.petsitters.org) and Pet Sitters International (336/983-9222; www.petsit.com).

✔ **The American Rabbit Breeders Association (ARBA)**
   If you're interested in a particular breed or information about breeding, showing, or breeders, check out www.arba.net.

✔ **Leith Petwerks**
   Cool, custom rabbit housing produced by Leith Petwerks. Call (800) 956-3576 or go to www.leithpetwerks.com.

✔ **Zooh Corner Rabbit Rescue**
   Their Web site, www.mybunny.org, is a treasure chest of care information and wisdom for anyone who loves rabbits.

Index

DOG BREEDS

Boxers For Dummies
0-7645-5285-6

German Shepherds For Dummies
0-7645-5280-5

Golden Retrievers For Dummies
0-7645-5267-8

Labrador Retrievers For Dummies
0-7645-5281-3

Pugs For Dummies
0-7645-54076-9

Retired Racing Greyhounds For Dummies
0-7645-5276-7

Siberian Huskies For Dummies
0-7645-5279-1

Yorkshire Terriers For Dummies
0-7645-6880-9

Also available:

Jack Russell Terriers For Dummies
(0-7645-5268-6)

Rottweilers For Dummies
(0-7645-5271-6)

Chihuahuas For Dummies
(0-7645-5284-8)

Dachshunds For Dummies
(0-7645-5289-9)

Pit Bulls For Dummies
(0-7645-5291-0)

DOG CARE, HEALTH, TRAINING, & BEHAVIOR

Puppies For Dummies
0-7645-5255-4

Dog Training For Dummies
0-7645-5286-4

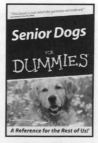

Senior Dogs For Dummies
0-7645-5818-8

Also available:

Choosing a Dog For Dummies
(0-7645-5310-0)

Dog Health & Nutrition For Dummies
(0-7645-5318-6)

Dog Tricks For Dummies
(0-7645-5287-2)

House Training For Dummies
(0-7645-5349-6)

Dogs For Dummies, 2nd Edition
(0-7645-5274-0)

FOR DUMMIES®

Pet care essentials in plain English

CATS & KITTENS

0-7645-5275-9

0-7645-4150-1

BIRDS

0-7645-5139-6

0-7645-5311-9

AMPHIBIANS & REPTILES

0-7645-2569-7

0-7645-5313-5

0-7645-5260-0

FISH & AQUARIUMS

0-7645-5156-6

0-7645-5340-2

SMALL ANIMALS

0-7645-5259-7

0-7645-0861-X